LARSON GEOMETRY

COMMON CORE **State Standards Curriculum Companion**

Student Edition

Ron Larson

Laurie Boswell

Timothy D. Kanold

Lee Stiff

HOLT McDOUGAL

HOUGHTON MIFFLIN HARCOURT

Printed in the U.S.A.

ISBN   978-0-547-61817-3

3 4 5 6 7 8 9 10 0877 20 19 18 17 16 15 14 13 12 11
4500305275   B C D E F G

Larson Geometry
Common Core State Standards
Curriculum Companion
Student Edition

Contents

4.2A Rigid Motions in the Plane

MATERIALS • graph paper • ruler • protractor

QUESTION Which transformations are rigid motions?

Transformations are functions that map points onto points. The result of transforming a figure is called its *image*. The original figure is called the *preimage*.

You can use function rules expressed with coordinate notation to describe some transformations.

EXPLORE 1 Use function rules for transformations

STEP 1 *Graph a triangle*

Graph the triangle whose vertices have the coordinates (1, 4), (3, −2), and (−1, 1).

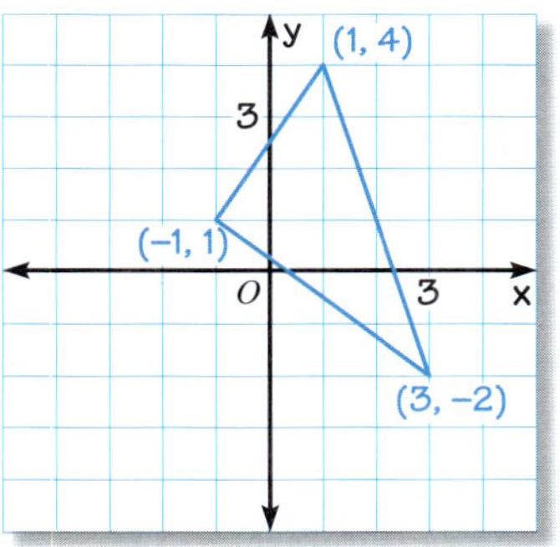

STEP 2 *Transform the triangle*

Transform each vertex of the triangle using this function rule:

$$(x, y) \rightarrow (x - 2, y - 1).$$

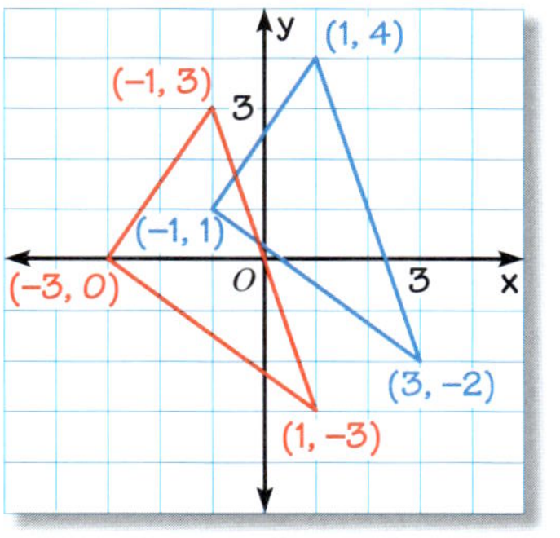

STEP 3 *Describe the transformation*

The transformation is a slide, or translation, 2 units left and 1 unit down. The image is congruent to the preimage.

STEP 4 *Repeat Steps 1–3 for different transformations*

For each function rule, draw a triangle and its image. Describe the transformation. Then tell whether the image is congruent to the preimage.

a. $(x, y) \rightarrow (-x, y)$

b. $(x, y) \rightarrow (2x, 2y)$

c. $(x, y) \rightarrow (-y, x)$

d. $(x, y) \rightarrow (x, 2y)$

A *rigid motion* is a transformation that preserves length and angle measure.

EXPLORE 2 Determine if a transformation is a rigid motion

STEP 1 Draw transformation

Draw a triangle and its image after a reflection. You may want to fold your paper along the line of reflection to trace the triangle.

STEP 2 Measure sides and angles

Use a protractor to measure the angles and a ruler to measure the side lengths of the preimage and image.

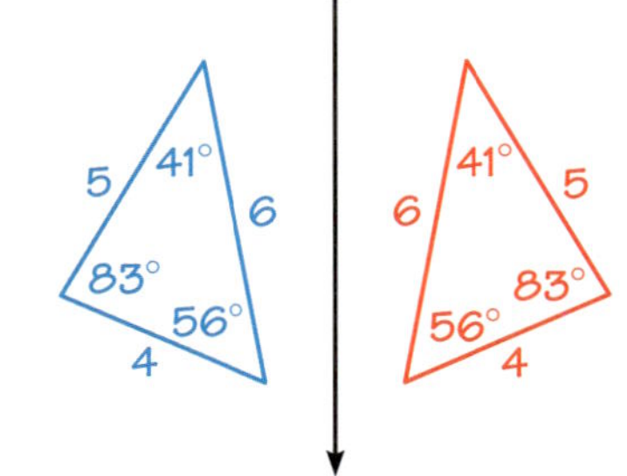
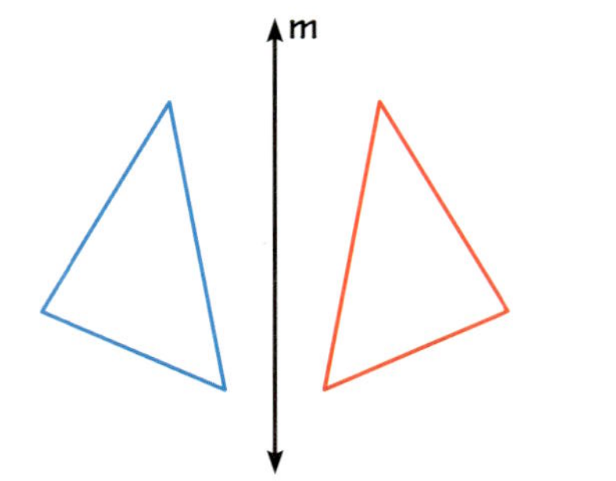

STEP 3 Tell whether it is a rigid motion

The reflection preserves lengths and angle measures. So, it is a rigid motion.

STEP 4 Repeat Steps 1–3 for different transformations

Draw a triangle and its image after an example of the transformation. Tell whether the transformation is a rigid motion.
 a. translation (slide) **b.** rotation (turn) **c.** dilation (enlargement)

DRAW CONCLUSIONS Use your observations to complete these exercises

1. Use coordinate notation to write a function rule that describes reflection in the x-axis. Is this transformation a rigid motion?

2. Use coordinate notation to write a function rule that describes a rotation of 90° clockwise about the origin. Is this transformation a rigid motion?

3. Use coordinate notation to write a function rule that describes a rotation of 180° about the origin. Is this transformation a rigid motion?

4. A triangle has vertices $(-1, 2)$, $(1, 3)$, and $(2, 0)$. What are the vertices of the image after a transformation described by the function rule $(x, y) \rightarrow (-2x, 3y)$? Is this transformation a rigid motion? *Explain.*

5. Which transformations in Explore 2 preserve length?

6. Which transformations in Explore 2 preserve angle measure?

7. Which transformations in Explore 2 are rigid motions?

8. If a transformation preserves area, is it always a rigid motion? If so, explain. If not, give a counterexample.

4.2B Relate Transformations and Congruence

Before	You identified congruent figures.
Now	You will use transformations to show congruence.
Why	So you can complete an architect's drawing, as in Ex. 28.

Key Vocabulary
• **rigid motion**

Transformations in the plane move or change a figure to produce a new figure. A **rigid motion** is a transformation that preserves length, angle measure, and area. A rigid motion is also called an *isometry*. *Translations, reflections,* and *rotations* are examples of rigid motions.

Recall that two figures are *congruent* if and only if the corresponding sides and the corresponding angles are congruent. Two geometric figures are congruent if and only if there is a rigid motion or a combination of rigid motions that move one of the figures onto the other.

READ VOCABULARY

Translations are also known as *slides*, reflections are also known as *flips*, and rotations are also known as *turns*.

KEY CONCEPT *For Your Notebook*

Congruent Figures and Transformations

Two figures are congruent if and only if one or more rigid motions can be used to move one figure onto the other. If any combination of translations, reflections, and rotations can be used to move one shape onto the other, the figures are congruent.

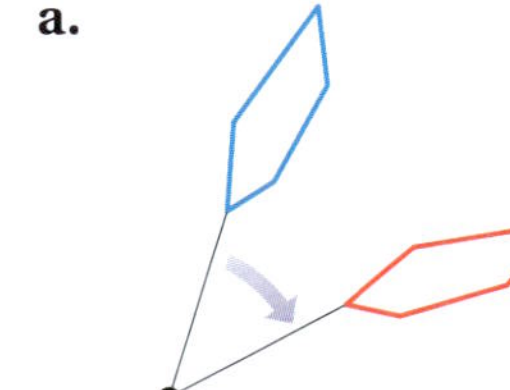

EXAMPLE 1 **Describe rigid motions to show congruence**

Describe the transformation(s) you can use to move the blue figure onto the red figure.

a.

b.

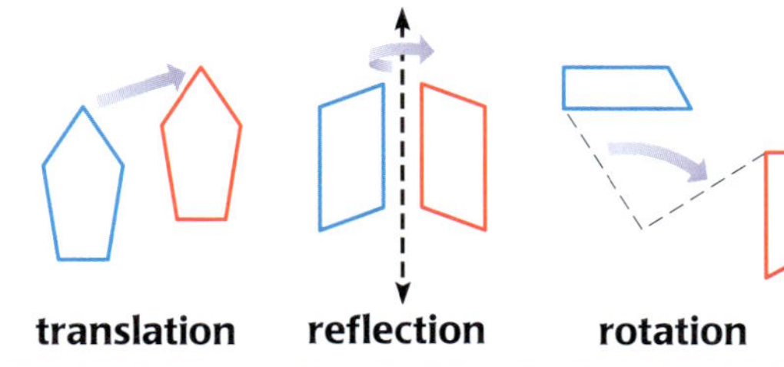

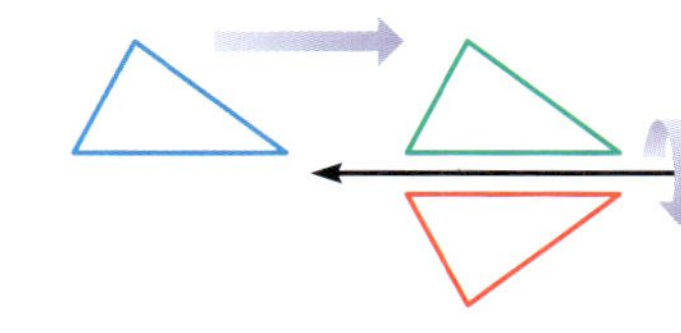

Solution

a. rotation about P

b. translation and then reflection

GUIDED PRACTICE   for Example 1

Describe the transformation(s) you can use to move the blue figure onto the red figure.

1.

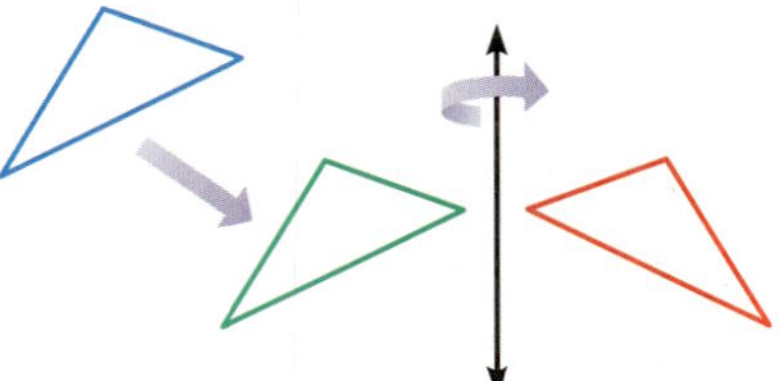

2.

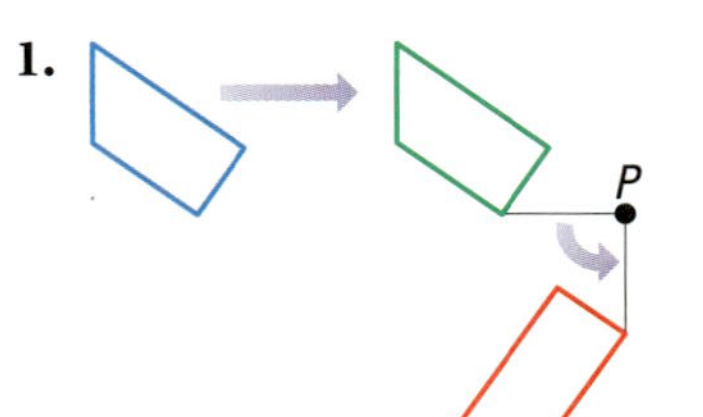

EXAMPLE 2   Show figures are not congruent

Explain why figure A and figure B are not congruent using transformations.

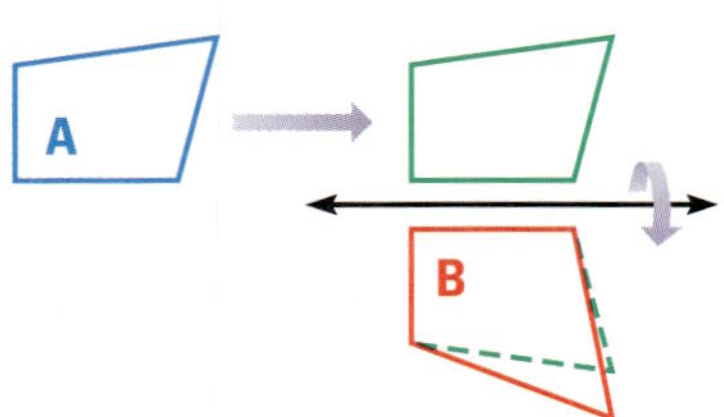

Solution

Translate and then reflect figure A to compare it to figure B. Although some of the corresponding sides are congruent, the corresponding angles are not all congruent. So, the figures are not congruent.

EXAMPLE 3   Move one figure in a pattern onto another

QUILTING The quilt shown is made using a repeating pattern.

a. Describe a transformation that moves figure A onto figure B.

b. Explain why figures C and D are congruent by using the marked angles and sides.

Solution

a. A translation or a rotation will move figure A onto figure B.

b. Figures C and D are congruent because all pairs of corresponding sides and all pairs of corresponding angles are congruent.

4.2B EXERCISES

HOMEWORK KEY

○ = **WORKED-OUT SOLUTIONS** for Exs. 11, 17, and 21

★ = **STANDARDIZED TEST PRACTICE** Exs. 2, 6–9, 21, 25, 28

SKILL PRACTICE

1. **VOCABULARY** Examples of transformations that are rigid motions are _?_ , _?_ , and _?_ .

2. ★ **WRITING** *Explain* why a transformation that maps one figure onto a congruent figure is a rigid motion.

EXAMPLE 1
on p. CC3
for Exs. 3–8

IDENTIFYING TRANSFORMATIONS Identify the transformation you can use to move the blue figure onto the red figure.

3.

4.

5.

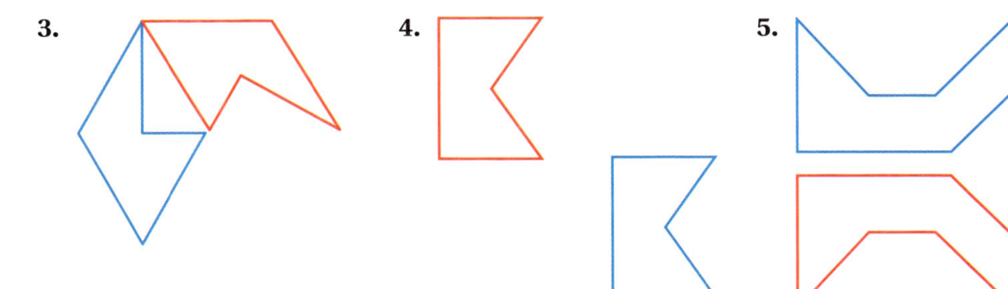

★ **OPEN-ENDED MATH** Copy the figure. Draw an example of the effect of the given transformation on the figure.

6. translation

7. reflection

8. rotation

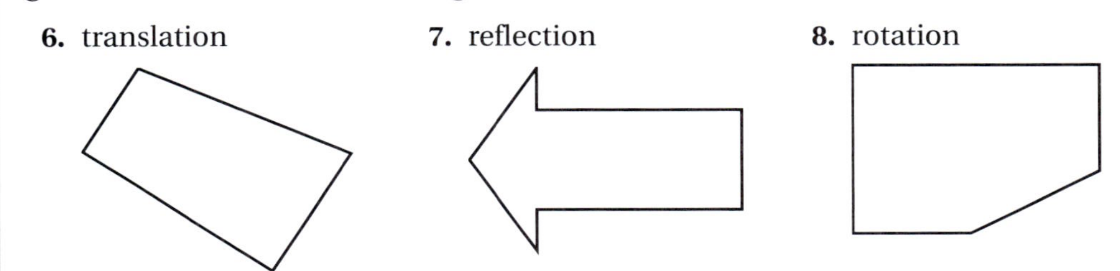

**EXAMPLES
2 AND 3**
on p. CC4
for Exs. 9–17

9. ★ **MULTIPLE CHOICE** Which is *not* an example of a rigid motion?

Ⓐ 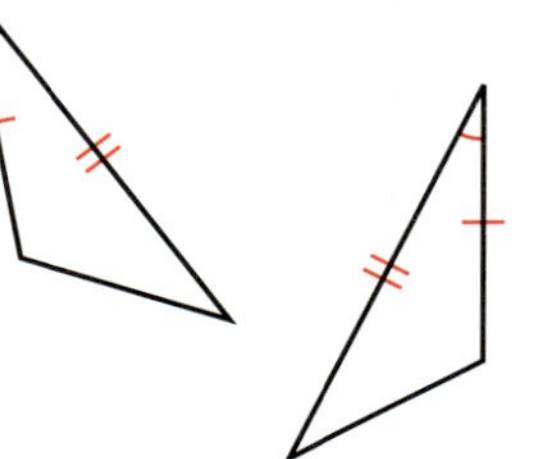

Ⓑ

Ⓒ 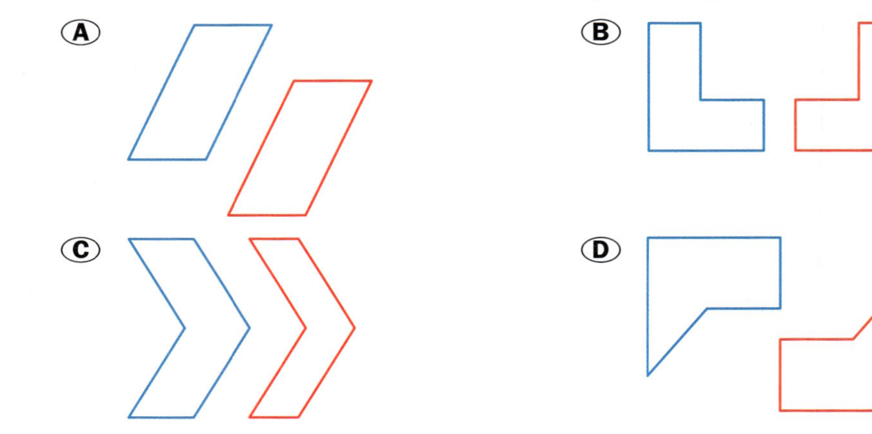

Ⓓ

SHOWING FIGURES CONGRUENT Tell whether a rigid motion can move the blue figure onto the red figure. If so, describe the transformation(s) that you can use. If not, explain why the figures are not congruent.

10.

11.

12.

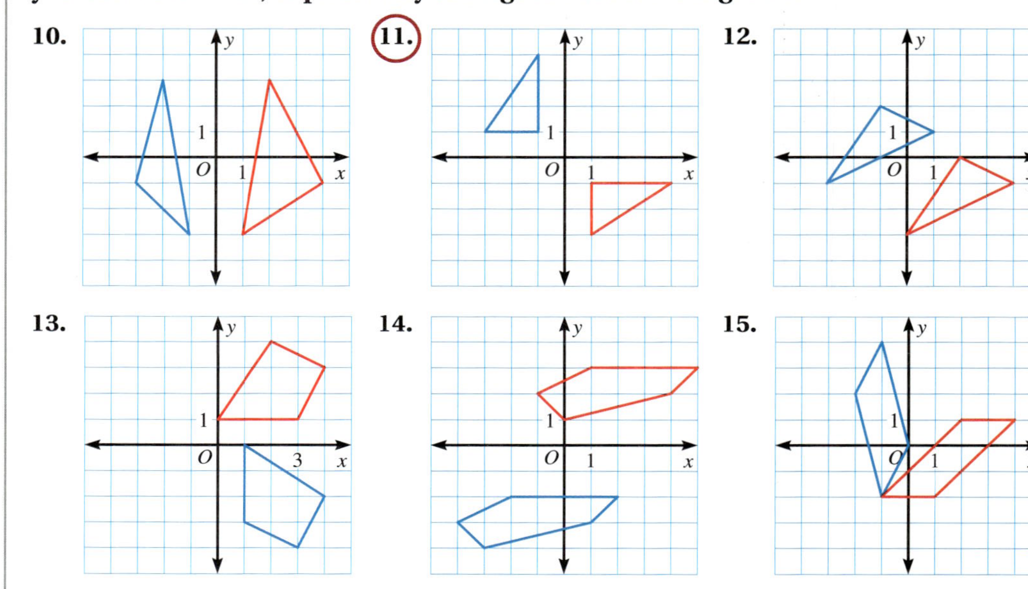

13.

14.

15.

16. Jerome describes a transformation in the coordinate plane using the notation $(x, y) \rightarrow (x + 3, y - 1)$. *Explain* why this is a rigid motion.

17. Jen describes a transformation in the coordinate plane using the notation $(x, y) \rightarrow (x - 1, 2y)$. *Explain* why this is *not* a rigid motion.

CHALLENGE Determine whether a rigid motion can move one triangle onto the other. Justify your answer.

18.

19. 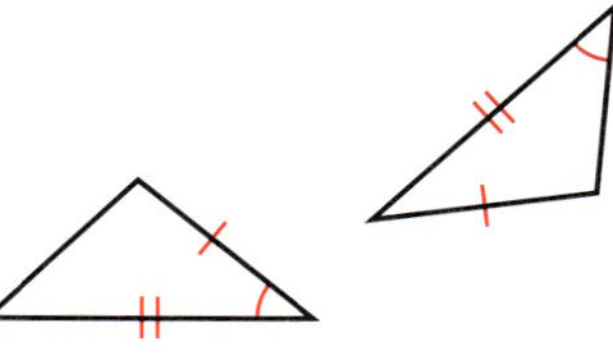

PROBLEM SOLVING

EXAMPLE 3
on p. CC4
for Exs. 20–26

20. **GAME SOFTWARE** In a game, the goal is to move shapes into congruent spaces where they will fit so that completed rows can be eliminated. Describe a combination of transformations that can be used to move game piece A into congruent space B.

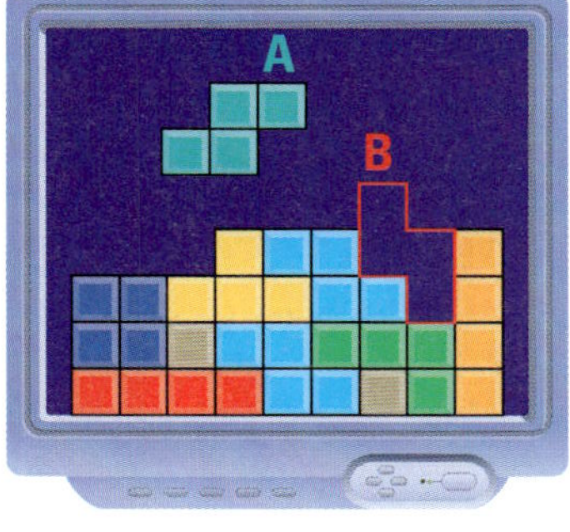

21. ★ **SHORT RESPONSE** Describe a way in which $\triangle ABC$ can be moved onto $\triangle DCB$ using just one transformation. Then describe a way in which $\triangle ABC$ can be moved onto $\triangle DCB$ using exactly two transformations.

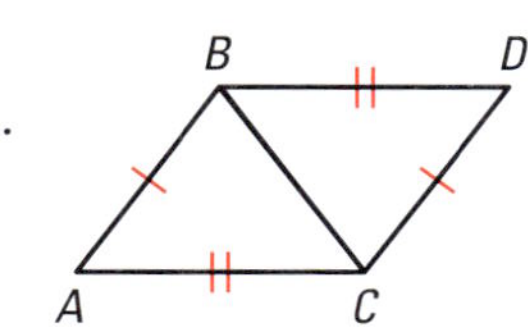

FLOORING Designs for floor tiles are shown below. Describe a rigid motion or combination of rigid motions that can be used to move the blue figure onto the red figure.

22. 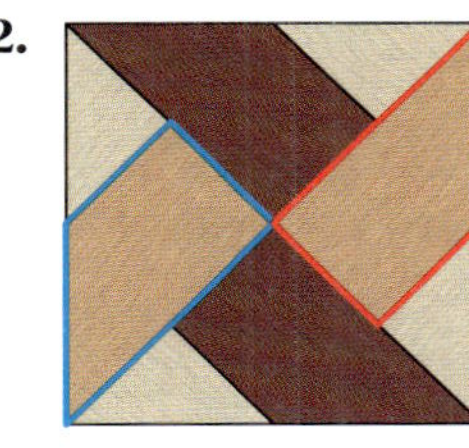

23.

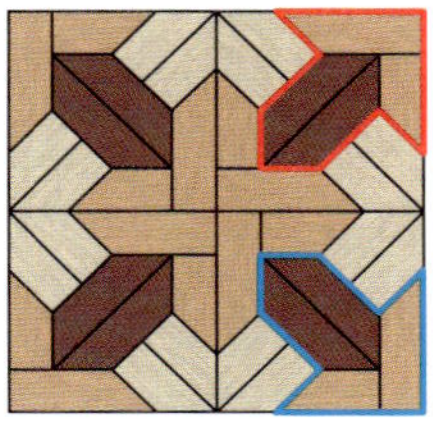

24.

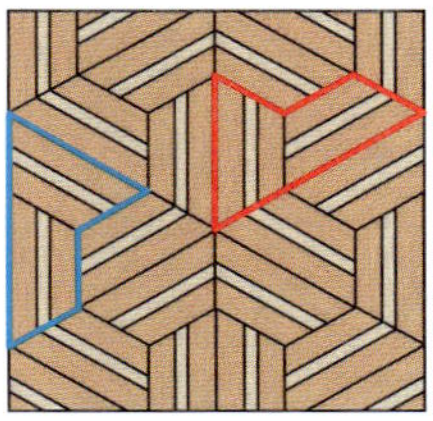

25. ★ **OPEN-ENDED MATH** Create a design using a combination of translations, reflections, or rotations.

26. **PENROSE TILES** The mathematician Roger Penrose investigated the patterns that can be made with tiles like the ones shown below.

   a. *Choose* two tiles of the same color in the pattern and show how to map one tile onto the other using a rotation.

   b. *Describe* the rotation angle and center.

   c. *Explain* how you calculated the rotation angle.

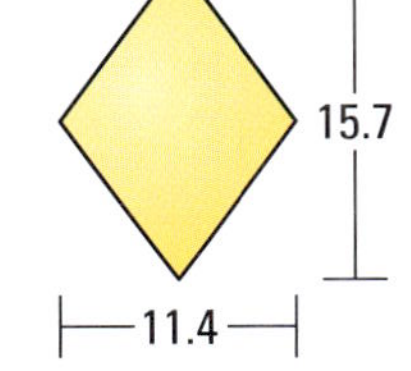

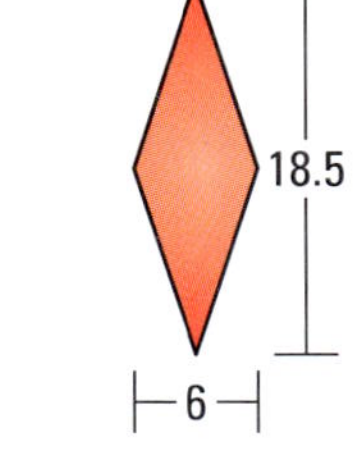

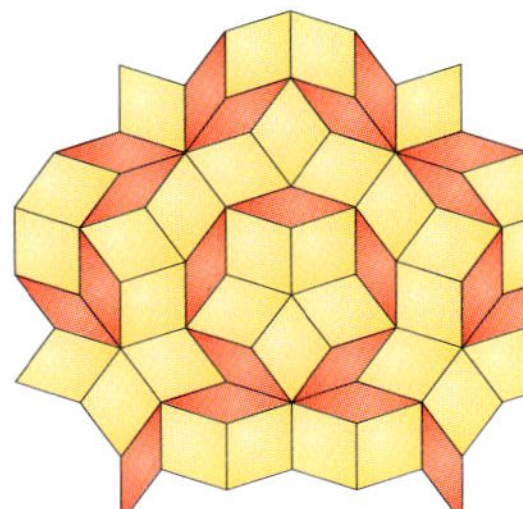

27. **CLOTHING DESIGN** A clothing manufacturer needs
two panels cut from cloth that are reflections of
each other to create part of a dress. *Explain* why
folding the fabric in half and cutting both pieces
together will produce the two panels.

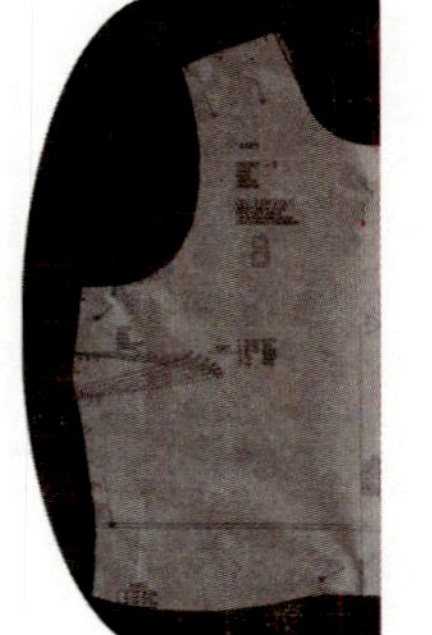

28. ★ **EXTENDED RESPONSE** The diagram shows an
architect's preliminary design for an A-frame house.

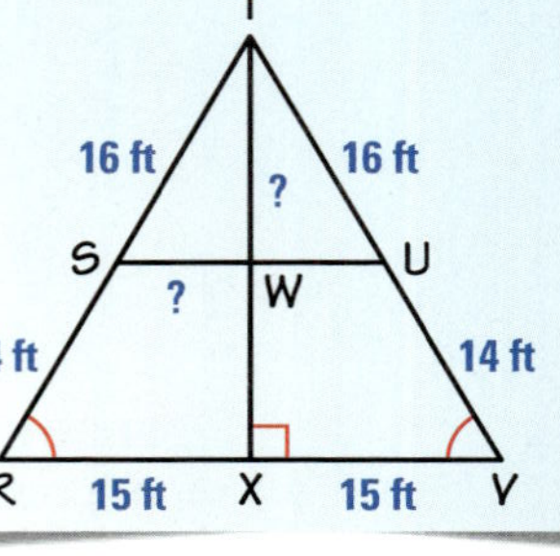

   a. **Interpret** Use rigid motions to explain how the
      architect knows $\triangle RTX \cong \triangle VTX$.

   b. **Reason** Explain how the architect can use rigid
      motions to conclude that $SW = UW$.

   c. **Calculate** The architect knows that the proportion
      $\dfrac{TS}{SW} = \dfrac{TR}{RX}$ is true. Find the lengths SW and TW.

29. **CHALLENGE** Draw examples of two congruent triangles that can be
mapped onto each other by the given transformation(s). Show the
lines(s) of reflection you use.

   a. exactly one reflection   b. exactly two reflections   c. exactly three reflections

MIXED REVIEW

**For Exercises 30–32, identify the property of congruent segments that
justifies the statement.** (*Lesson 2.6*)

PREVIEW
Prepare for
Lesson 4.3
in Exs. 30–32

30. If $\overline{AB} \cong \overline{CD}$, then $\overline{CD} \cong \overline{AB}$.

31. For any segment AB, $\overline{AB} \cong \overline{AB}$.

32. If $\overline{AB} \cong \overline{CD}$ and then $\overline{CD} \cong \overline{EF}$, then $\overline{AB} \cong \overline{EF}$.

33. A top view of the path between two buildings is shown.
Use the Alternate Interior Angles Theorem to prove that
$\angle 1 \cong \angle 4$. (*Lessons 2.6 and 3.2*)

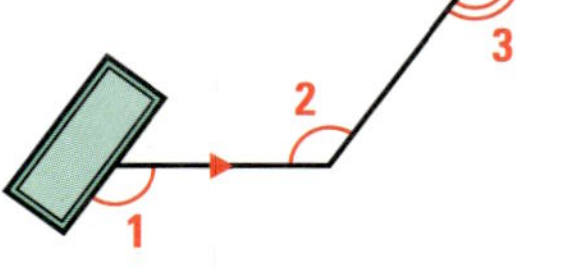

Find the slope of the line that passes through the points. (*Lesson 3.4*)

34. $(0, 0)$, $(3, 12)$ 35. $(-1, 4)$, $(0, 3)$ 36. $(3, -2)$, $(5, -2)$

37. Write an equation of the line passing through the point $(-1, -2)$ that is
parallel to the line with the equation $y = -x + 1$. (*Lesson 3.5*)

38. Write an equation of the line passing through the point $(2, 3)$ that is
perpendicular to the line with the equation $y = x - 4$. (*Lesson 3.5*)

Mastering *the* Standards

for Mathematical Practice

The topics described in the Standards for Mathematical Content will vary from year to year. However, the *way* in which you learn, study, and think about mathematics will not. The Standards for Mathematical Practice describe skills that you will use in all of your math courses.

Mathematical Practices

1. *Make sense of problems and persevere in solving them.*
2. *Reason abstractly and quantitatively.*
3. *Construct viable arguments and critique the reasoning of others.*
4. *Model with mathematics.*
5. *Use appropriate tools strategically.*
6. *Attend to precision.*
7. *Look for and make use of structure.*
8. *Look for and express regularity in repeated reasoning.*

❶ Make sense of problems and persevere in solving them.

Mathematically proficient students start by explaining to themselves the meaning of a problem... They analyze givens, constraints, relationships, and goals. They make conjectures about the form... of the solution and plan a solution pathway...

In your book

Verbal Models and the **Problem Solving Plan** help you translate the information in a problem into a model and then analyze your solution.

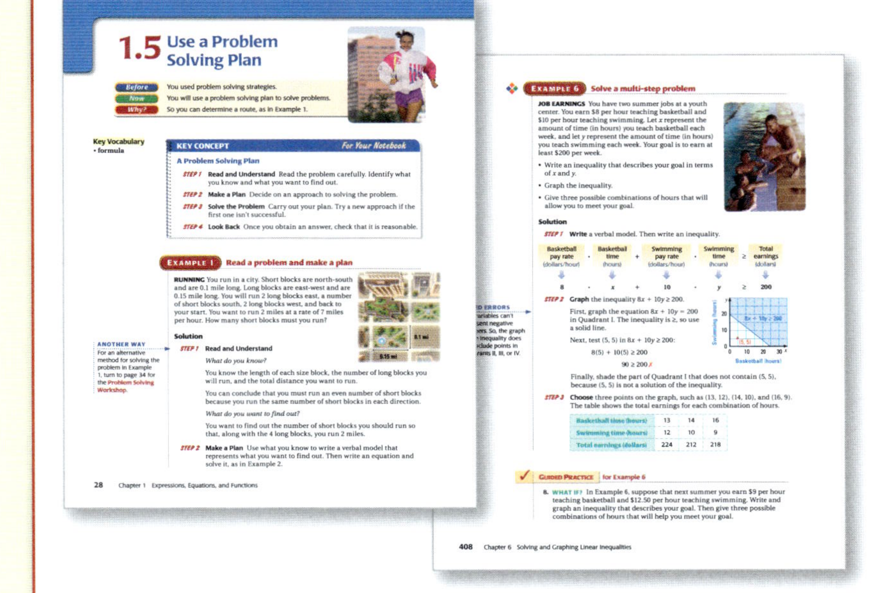

1.5 Use a Problem Solving Plan

Before You used problem solving strategies.
Now You will use a problem solving plan to solve problems.
Why? So you can determine a route, as in Example 1.

Key Vocabulary
• formula

KEY CONCEPT *For Your Notebook*

A Problem Solving Plan

STEP 1 **Read and Understand** Read the problem carefully. Identify what you know and what you want to find out.

STEP 2 **Make a Plan** Decide on an approach to solving the problem.

STEP 3 **Solve the Problem** Carry out your plan. Try a new approach if the first one isn't successful.

STEP 4 **Look Back** Once you obtain an answer, check that it is reasonable.

EXAMPLE 1 **Read a problem and make a plan**

RUNNING You run in a city. Short blocks are north-south and are 0.1 mile long. Long blocks are east-west and are 0.15 mile long. You will run 2 long blocks east, a number of short blocks south, 2 long blocks west, and back to your start. You want to run 2 miles at a rate of 7 miles per hour. How many short blocks must you run?

Solution

ANOTHER WAY
For an alternative method for solving the problem in Example 1, turn to page 34 for the Problem Solving Workshop.

STEP 1 **Read and Understand**

What do you know?

You know the length of each size block, the number of long blocks you will run, and the total distance you want to run.

You can conclude that you must run an even number of short blocks because you run the same number of short blocks in each direction.

What do you want to find out?

You want to find out the number of short blocks you should run so that, along with the 4 long blocks, you run 2 miles.

STEP 2 **Make a Plan** Use what you know to write a verbal model that represents what you want to find out. Then write an equation and solve it, as in Example 2.

28 Chapter 1 Expressions, Equations, and Functions

EXAMPLE 6 **Solve a multi-step problem**

JOB EARNINGS You have two summer jobs at a youth center. You earn $8 per hour teaching basketball and $10 per hour teaching swimming. Let x represent the amount of time (in hours) you teach basketball each week, and let y represent the amount of time (in hours) you teach swimming each week. Your goal is to earn at least $200 per week.

• Write an inequality that describes your goal in terms of x and y.
• Graph the inequality.
• Give three possible combinations of hours that will allow you to meet your goal.

Solution

STEP 1 **Write** a verbal model. Then write an inequality.

Basketball pay rate (dollars/hour)		Basketball time (hours)		Swimming pay rate (dollars/hour)		Swimming time (hours)		Total earnings (dollars)
8	·	x	+	10	·	y	≥	200

STEP 2 **Graph** the inequality $8x + 10y \geq 200$.

First, graph the equation $8x + 10y = 200$ in Quadrant I. The inequality is ≥, so use a solid line.

Next, test (5, 5) in $8x + 10y \geq 200$:

$$8(5) + 10(5) \geq 200$$
$$90 \geq 200 \ ✗$$

Finally, shade the part of Quadrant I that does not contain (5, 5), because (5, 5) is not a solution of the inequality.

STEP 3 **Choose** three points on the graph, such as (13, 12), (14, 10), and (16, 9). The table shows the total earnings for each combination of hours.

Basketball time (hours)	13	14	16
Swimming time (hours)	12	10	9
Total earnings (dollars)	224	212	218

GUIDED PRACTICE for Example 6

8. **WHAT IF?** In Example 6, suppose that next summer you earn $9 per hour teaching basketball and $12.50 per hour teaching swimming. Write and graph an inequality that describes your goal. Then give three possible combinations of hours that will help you meet your goal.

408 Chapter 6 Solving and Graphing Linear Inequalities

4.5 Rigid Motions and Congruence

MATERIALS · compass · straightedge

QUESTION How does triangle congruence follow from rigid motions?

In the following constructions, rigid motions will be used to explain the criteria for triangle congruence.

EXPLORE 1 Construct triangles from three segments (SSS)

Given three segments, like the ones at the right, use these steps to construct triangles with those three side lengths.

STEP 1 *Copy a segment* Copy one of the line segments. In the diagram, the longest segment is copied. Label the endpoints *A* and *B*.

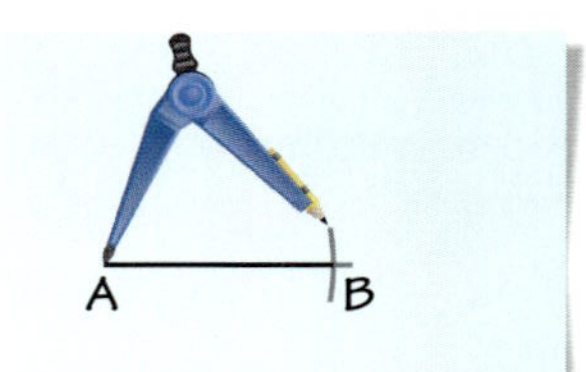

STEP 2 *Draw circles* At both endpoints of the segment, draw circles using the other two given side lengths as radii.

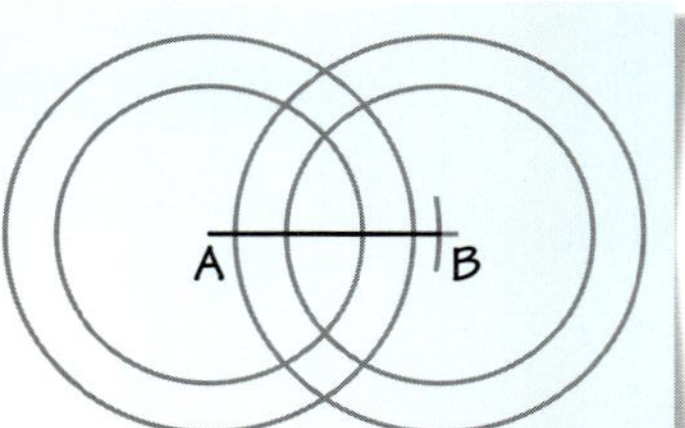

STEP 3 *Find vertices* Identify the four places where circles of different radii intersect. Label the points *C*, *D*, *E*, and *F*.

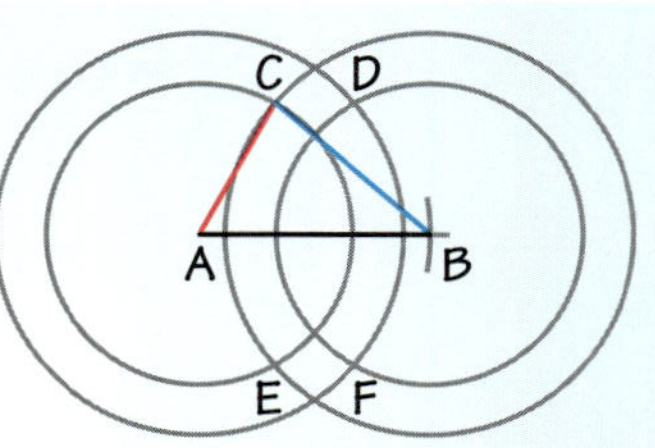

STEP 4 *Draw triangles* Draw △*ABC*, △*ABE*, △*BAD*, and △*BAF*.

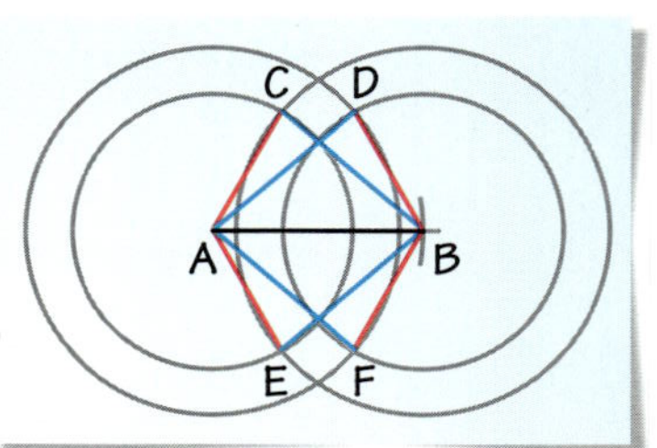

EXPLORE 2 **Construct triangles from two segments and an angle (SAS)**

Given two segments and one angle, like the ones at the right, use these steps
to construct triangles with those side lengths and included angle.

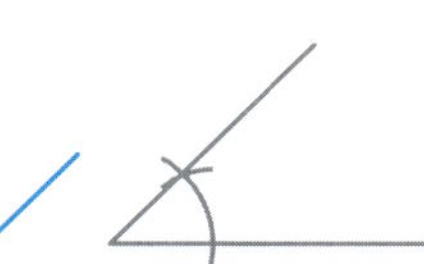

STEP 1 *Copy a segment* Copy one of the line segments. Label the
endpoints A and B.

STEP 2 *Copy angles* Use the copy and
angle construction to make two
copies of the angle at point A,
one above and one below the
segment. Then do the same
thing at point B.

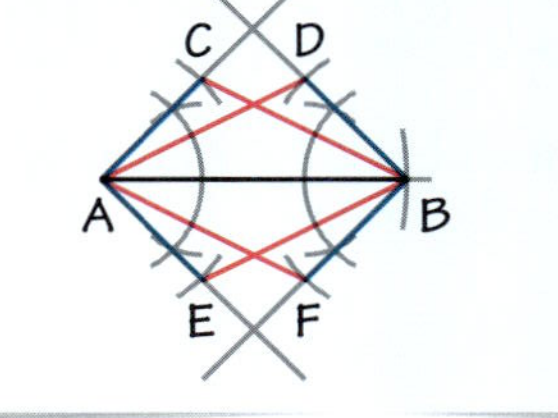

STEP 3 *Copy segments* Using the other
given side length as radius,
draw arcs with centers A and B.
Label where the arcs intersect
the lines from Step 2 as points
C, D, E, and F.

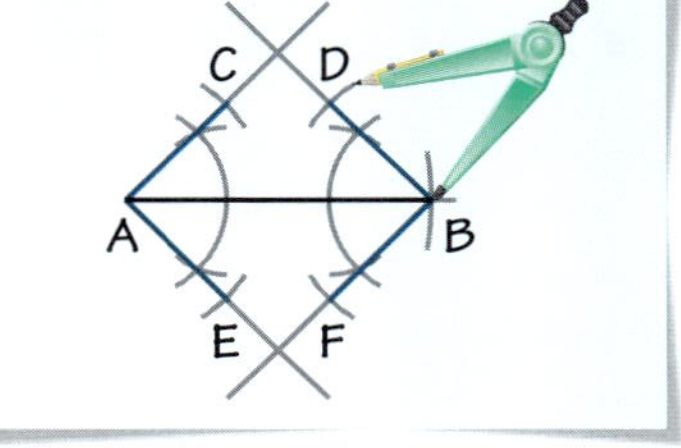

STEP 4 *Draw triangles* Draw $\triangle ABC$,
$\triangle ABE$, $\triangle BAD$, and $\triangle BAF$.

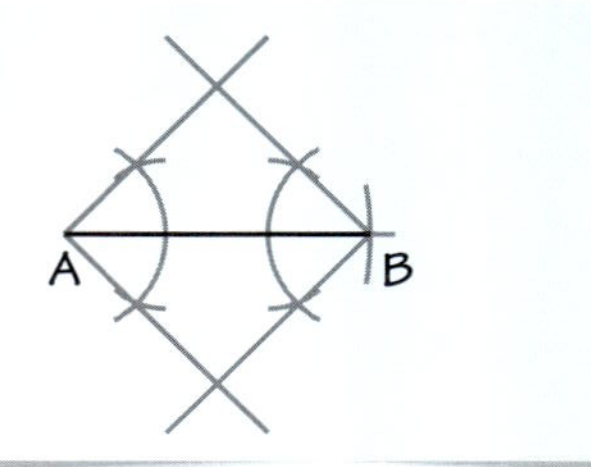

DRAW CONCLUSIONS **Use your observations to complete these exercises**

1. Refer to your work in Explore 1 and 2. Describe a rigid motion you can
   use to show that $\triangle ABC \cong \triangle ABE$ and $\triangle BAD \cong \triangle BAF$.

2. Refer to your work in Explore 1 and 2. Describe a rigid motion you can
   use to show that $\triangle ABC \cong \triangle BAD$ and $\triangle ABE \cong \triangle BAF$.

3. Is there a rigid motion you can use to show that $\triangle ABC \cong \triangle BAF$ and
   $\triangle ABD \cong \triangle BAE$? If so, describe it.

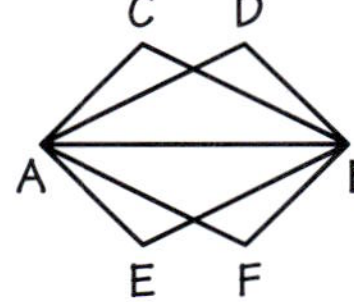

4. What can you conclude about the 4 triangles in each Explore?

5. Follow steps like those in Explore 1 and 2 to construct triangles given
   two angles and an included side (ASA). Can you use rigid motions to
   show these triangles are all congruent? *Explain.*

6.3A Explore Properties of Dilations

MATERIALS • graph paper • ruler • protractor

QUESTION   How do dilations affect lines, segments, and angles?

Dilations are non-rigid transformations that map points to points in the coordinate plane. A function rule in coordinate notation for a dilation with center at the origin is $(x, y) \rightarrow (kx, ky)$.

The ratio of the length of an image segment to its corresponding preimage segment is the *scale factor k* of the dilation.

EXPLORE   Draw a dilation of a triangle in the plane

STEP 1

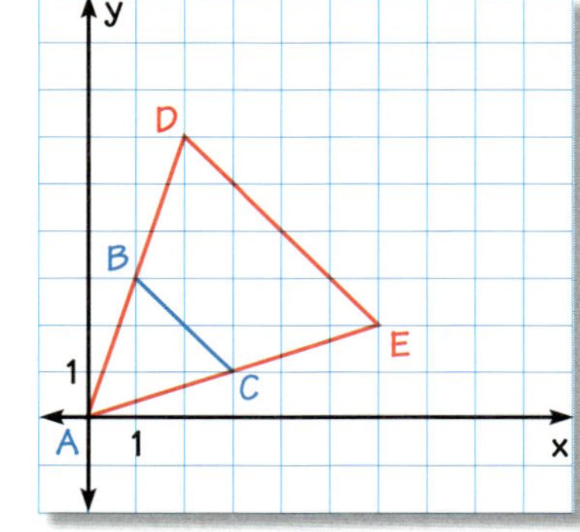

STEP 2

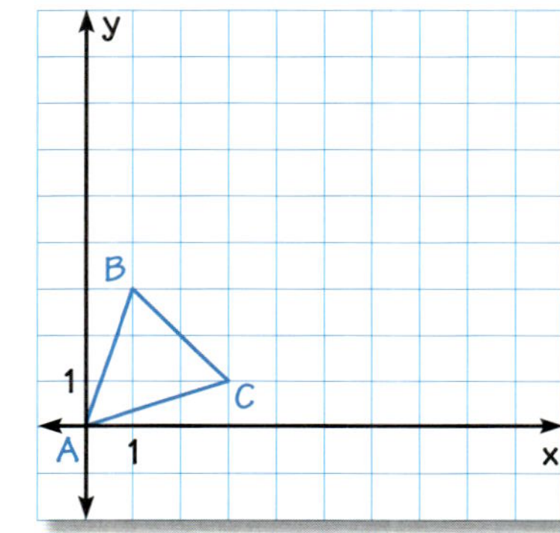

Graph a triangle Graph a triangle in a coordinate plane one of whose vertices is (0, 0).

Dilate the triangle Graph a dilation of the triangle with scale factor 2 and centered at the origin.

DRAW CONCLUSIONS   Use your observations to complete these exercises

1. Measure the sides and angles of $\triangle ABC$ and $\triangle ADE$. Tell whether the dilation preserves lengths or angle measures.

2. Compare the ratios $\dfrac{DE}{BC}$, $\dfrac{DA}{BA}$, and $\dfrac{EA}{CA}$. What do you notice?

3. What is the effect of the dilation on the center of dilation? *Explain.*

4. How is $\overleftrightarrow{AB}$ related to $\overleftrightarrow{AD}$? How does a dilation affect a line that passes through the center of dilation? *Explain.*

5. How is $\overleftrightarrow{BC}$ related to $\overleftrightarrow{DE}$? How does a dilation affect a line that does not pass through the center of dilation? *Explain.*

6.3B Relate Transformations and Similarity

Before	You identified rigid motions in the plane.
Now	You will identify similarity transformations called dilations.
Why?	So you can find the dimensions of a scale drawing, as in Ex. 30.

Key Vocabulary
- dilation
- scale factor

A **dilation** is a transformation that preserves angle measures and results in an image with lengths proportional to the preimage lengths.

The ratio of the lengths of the corresponding sides of the image and the preimage is called the **scale factor** of the dilation. Dilations can also be called *similarity transformations*.

KEY CONCEPT *For Your Notebook*

Dilations and Similarity

If a dilation can be used to move one figure onto another, the two figures are similar.

$$\triangle ABC \sim \triangle XYZ$$

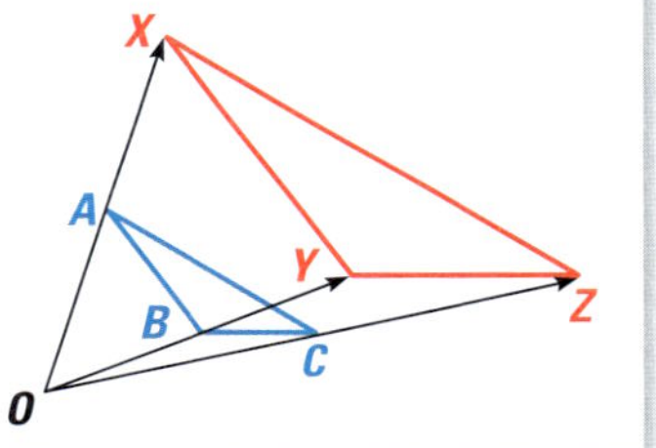

EXAMPLE 1 Describe a dilation

$\triangle FEG$ is similar to $\triangle FDH$. **Describe the dilation that moves $\triangle FEG$ onto $\triangle FDH$.**

Solution

The figure shows a dilation with center F.
The scale factor is 2 because the ratio of FH to FG is 20 : 10, or 2 : 1.

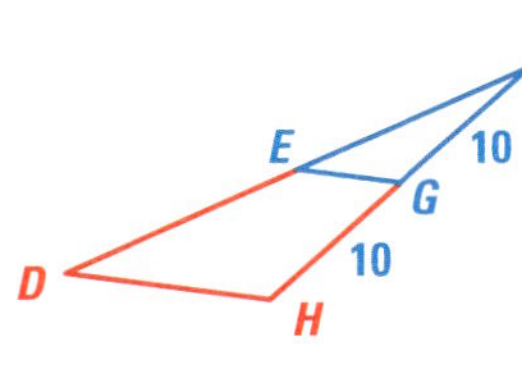

KEY CONCEPT *For Your Notebook*

Combining Dilations and Rigid Motions

If a dilation followed by any combination of rigid motions can be used to move one figure onto the other, the two figures are similar.

$\triangle ABC \sim \triangle DEF$ and $\triangle DEF \cong \triangle GHJ$,
so $\triangle ABC \sim \triangle GHJ$.

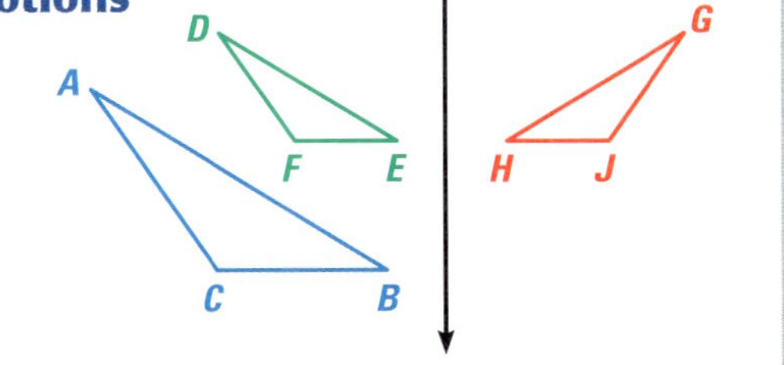

EXAMPLE 2 Describe a combination of transformations

$\triangle ABC$ is similar to $\triangle FGE$. Describe a combination
of transformations that moves $\triangle ABC$ onto $\triangle FGE$.

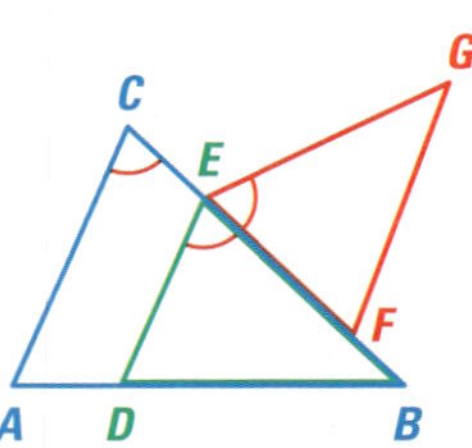

Solution

A dilation with center B and scale factor $\frac{2}{3}$ moves
$\triangle ABC$ onto $\triangle DBE$.

Then a rotation of $\triangle DBE$ with center E moves $\triangle DBE$ onto
$\triangle FGE$. The angle of rotation is equal to the measure of $\angle C$.

GUIDED PRACTICE for Examples 1 and 2

The two figures are similar. Describe the transformation(s) that move
the blue figure onto the red figure.

1.

2.

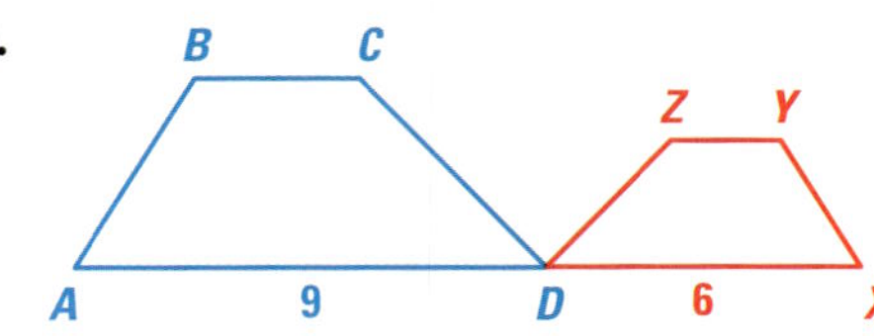

EXAMPLE 3 Use transformations to show figures are not similar

Use transformations to explain why
$ABCDE$ and $KLQRP$ are *not* similar.

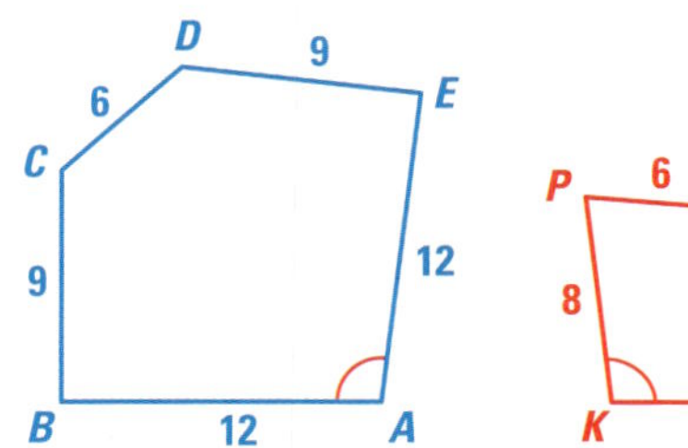

Solution

Corresponding sides in the pentagons are
proportional with a scale factor of $\frac{2}{3}$.

However, this does not necessarily mean
the pentagons are similar.

A dilation with center A and scale
factor $\frac{2}{3}$ moves *ABCDE* onto *AFGHJ*.
Then a reflection moves *AFGHJ*
onto *KLMNP*.

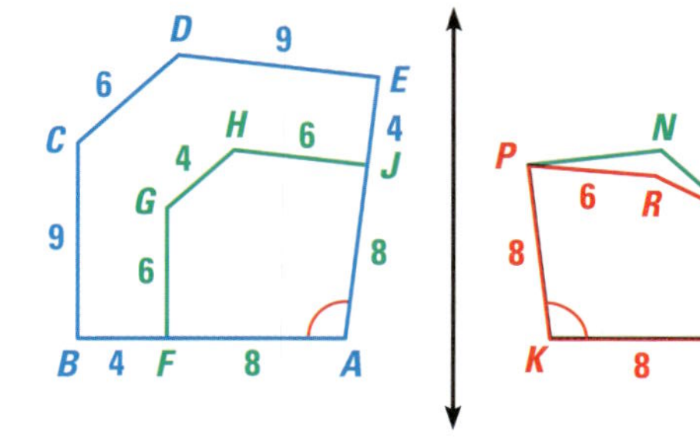

KLMNP does not exactly coincide with *KLQRP*, because not all of the
corresponding angles are congruent. (Only $\angle A$ and $\angle K$ are congruent.)
Since angle measure is not preserved, the two pentagons are not similar.

EXAMPLE 4 Use similar figures

GRAPHIC DESIGN A design for a party mask is made using all equilateral triangles and a scale factor of $\frac{1}{2}$.

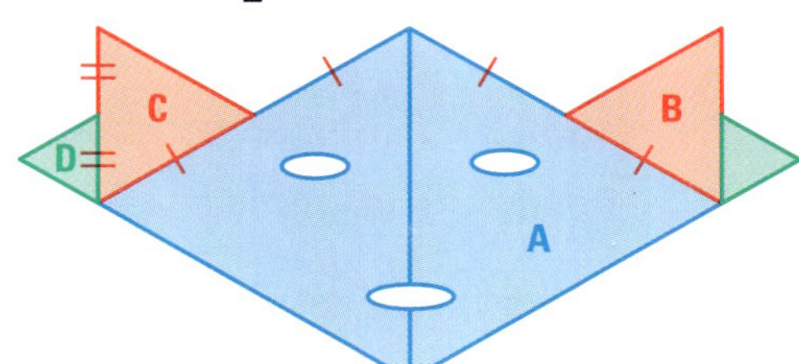

a. Describe transformations that move triangle A onto triangle B.

b. Describe why triangles C and D are similar by using the given infomation.

Solution

a. The figure shows a dilation with scale factor $\frac{1}{2}$ followed by a clockwise rotation of 60°.

b. Triangles C and D are similar because all pairs of corresponding sides are proportional with a ratio of $\frac{1}{2}$ and all pairs of corresponding angles of equilateral triangles have the same measure.

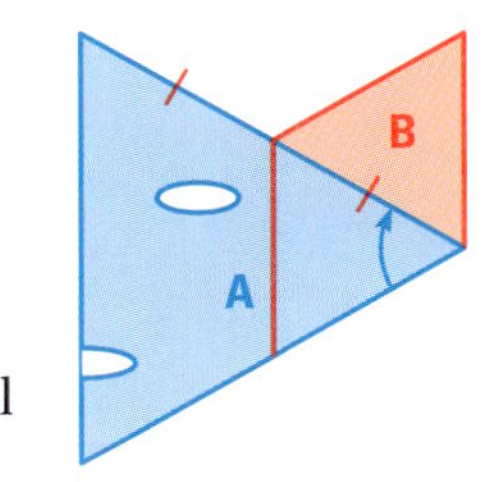

GUIDED PRACTICE for Examples 3 and 4

Refer to the floor tile designs shown below. In each design, the red shape is a regular hexagon.

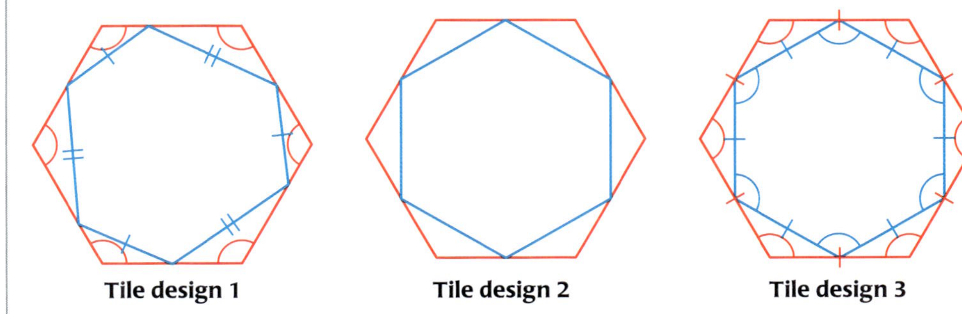

| Tile design 1 | Tile design 2 | Tile design 3 |

3. Tile design 1 is made using two hexagons. *Explain* why the red and blue hexagons are not similar.

4. Tile design 2 is made using two similar geometric shapes. *Describe* the transformations that move the blue hexagon to the red hexagon.

5. Tile design 3 shows congruent angles and sides. *Explain* why the red and blue hexagons are similar, using the given information.

6. If the lengths of all the sides of one polygon are proportional to the lengths of all the corresponding sides of another polygon, must the polygons be similar? *Explain.*

6.3B EXERCISES

SKILL PRACTICE

1. **VOCABULARY** Draw an example of a dilation.

2. ★ **WRITING** Describe the results of a similarity transformation.

EXAMPLE 1
on p. CC13
for Exs. 1–6

DESCRIBING DILATIONS Describe the dilation that moves the blue figure onto the red figure.

3. 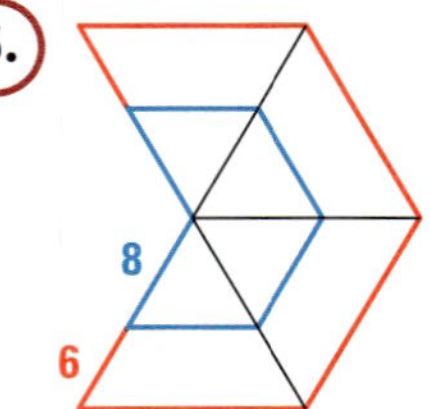

4. 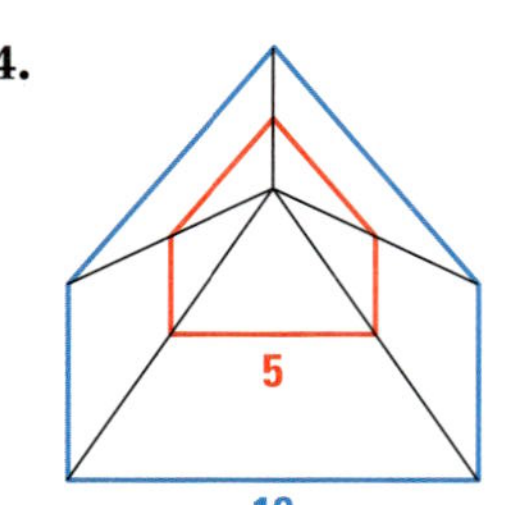

5. 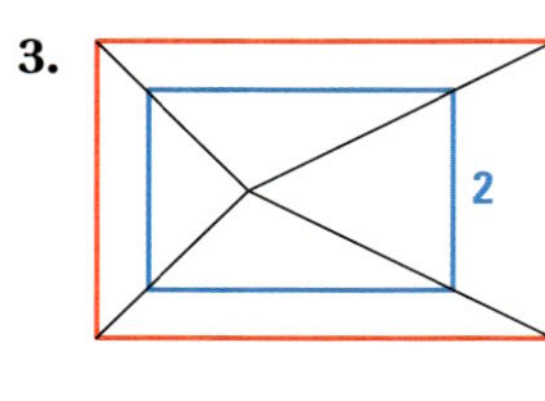

6. ★ **WRITING** Jenny described a transformation in the coordinate plane using the notation $(x, y) \rightarrow (3x, 3y)$. Explain why her transformation is a dilation with center at the origin.

EXAMPLE 2
on p. CC14
for Exs. 7–9

DRAWING SIMILARITY TRANSFORMATIONS Copy the figure. Draw an example of the given similarity transformation of the figure with center O.

7. 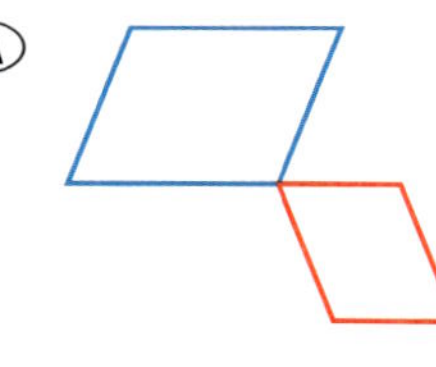

dilation

8. 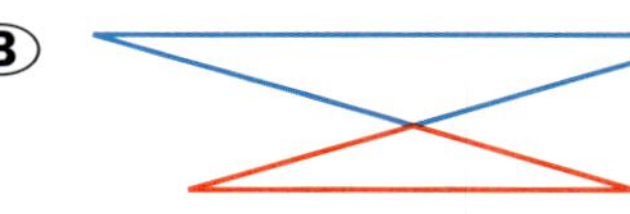

dilation then reflection

9. 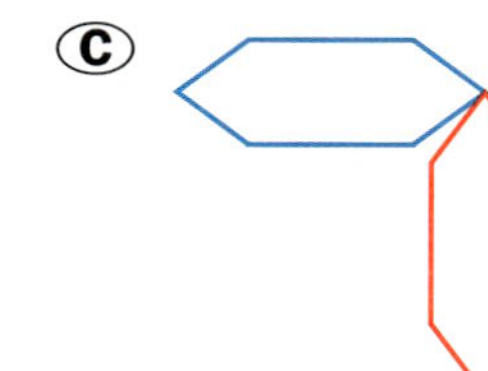

dilation then rotation

EXAMPLE 3
on p. CC14
for Ex. 10–12

10. ★ **MULTIPLE CHOICE** Which of the following transformations does *not* involve dilation?

Ⓐ 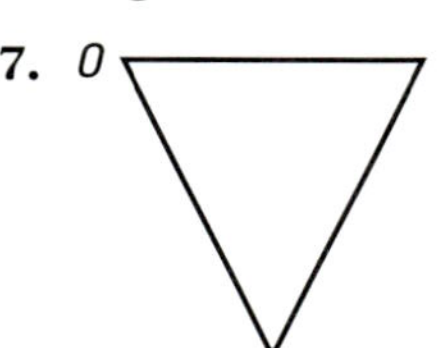

Ⓑ 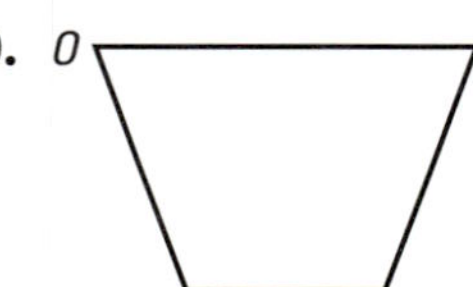

Ⓒ 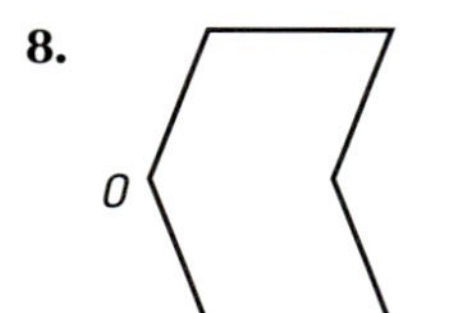

Ⓓ 

IDENTIFYING DILATIONS The red figure is the image of the blue figure under a transformation. Tell whether the transformation involves a dilation. If so, give the scale factor of the dilation.

11. 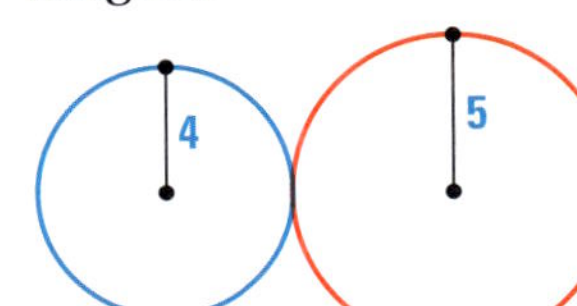

12. 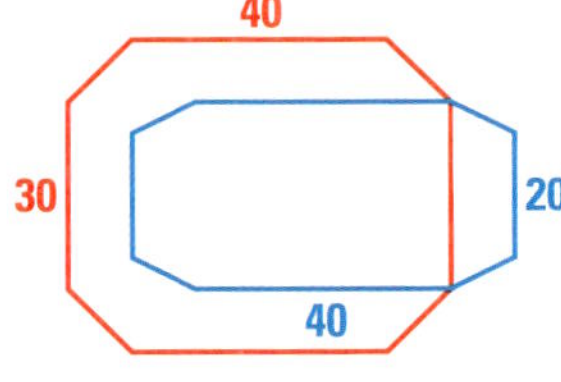

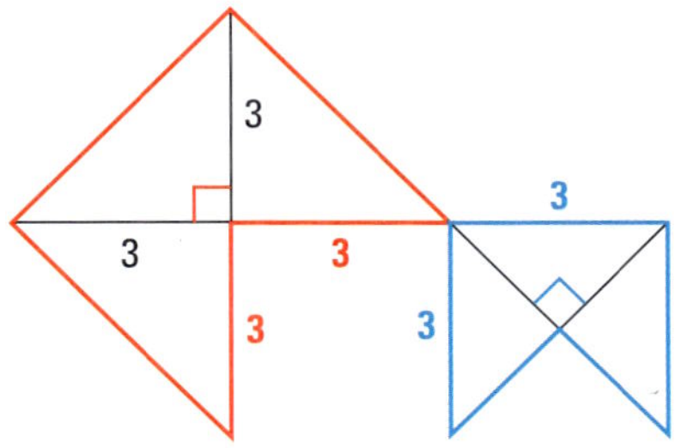

COMBINING TRANSFORMATIONS Coordinates of the vertices of a preimage and image figure are given. Describe the transformations that move the first figure onto the second.

13. $O(0, 0), B(0, 3), C(2, 0); O(0, 0), D(0, -6), E(4, 0)$

14. $O(0, 0), P(0, 8), Q(6, 0); O(0, 0), R(4, 0), S(0, -3)$

15. $J(-4, 0), K(0, 4), L(6, 0); L(6, 0), M(0, 6), N(-9, 0)$

16. $A(-6, 0), B(0, 6), C(9, 0), D(0, -15); W(0, -2), X(-2, 0), Y(0, 3), Z(5, 0)$

17. ★ **SHORT RESPONSE** A fractal called the *Sierpinski triangle* can be imagined by thinking of an infinite sequence of stages, the first of which are shown below. Calculate the side lengths of the light blue triangles in Stages 1, 2, and 3. Then describe the 3 dilations you can apply to any stage to generate the next stage.

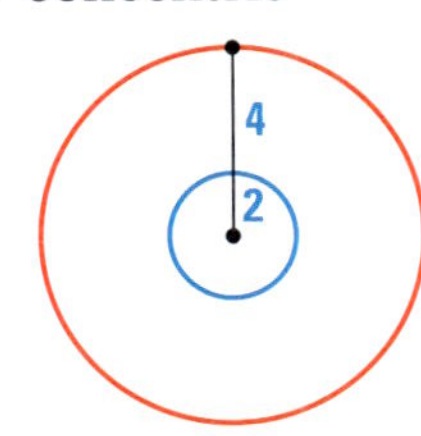

Stage 0   Stage 1   Stage 2   Stage 3

SIMILARITY OF CIRCLES Prove the circles are similar by finding a center and scale factor of a dilation that moves the blue circle onto the red circle.

18. concentric

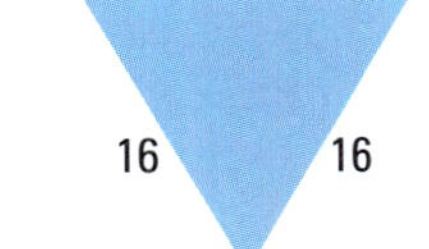

19. intersecting

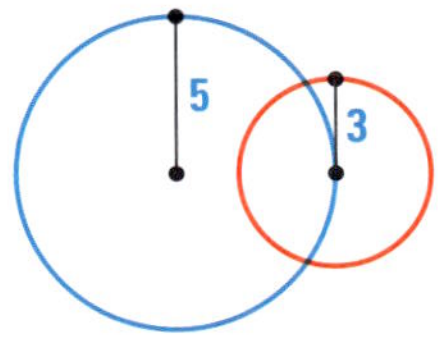

20. tangent

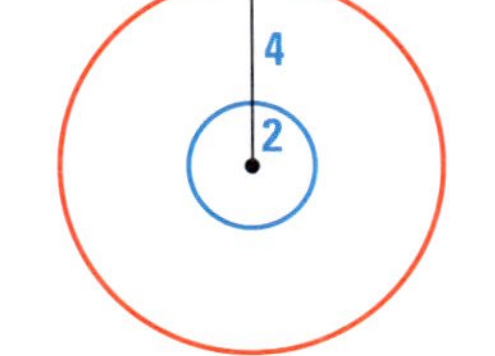

21. not intersecting

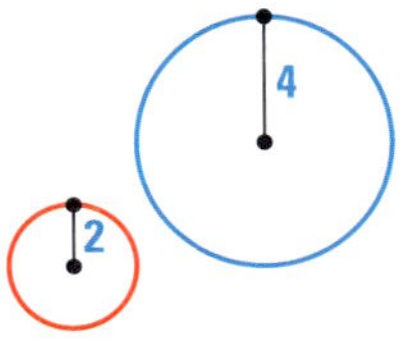

22. **CHALLENGE** The dilation of a rectangle has a scale factor of 4 to 1.

   a. Describe the effect of the dilation on the perimeter of the rectangle.

   b. Describe the effect of the dilation on the area of the rectangle.

PROBLEM SOLVING

EXAMPLE 4
on p. CC15
for Exs. 23–28

23. **TEXTILES** A cloth purse maker uses a pattern for a small bag. The maker wants to start making a similar bag that is exactly twice as big as the small one and has the same design. Explain how you might efficiently create the design for the large bag.

24. **GRAPHIC ARTS** Describe how using an overhead projector involves dilations when creating a larger image that can be traced onto a poster.

25. **CRAFTS** A rug design uses similar triangles that become larger on one side while getting smaller on the other side. What transformations are used to move figure A onto figure B?

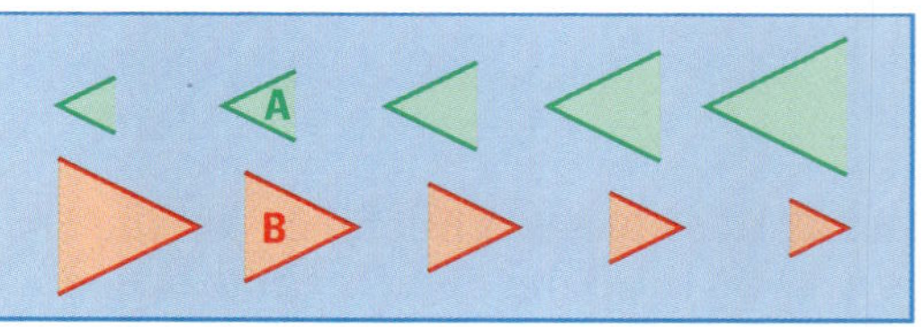

26. ★ **OPEN-ENDED** Create a design using a combination of dilations and other transformations.

27. **TOY IDEA** A flashlight has a removable cap with a picture on it. When the flashlight is on, the bug can be projected onto a wall. Using the information in the diagram below, find the scale factor of the dilation. Then calculate the height of the bug projected onto the wall.

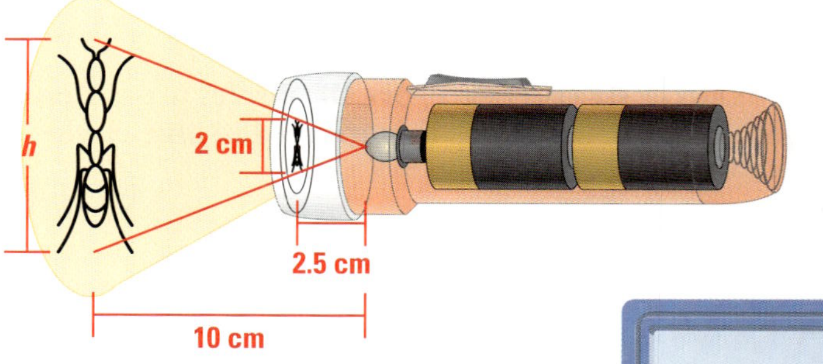

28. **ANIMATION** You are designing an animated lightning bolt on a computer screen. You want the distance of each bolt from P to be $\frac{1}{5}$ greater than the distance of the previous bolt. Describe the transformation that moves each bolt to the next larger bolt.

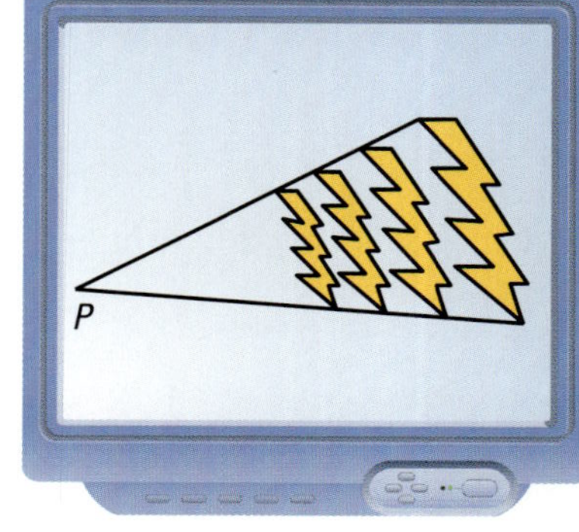

29. **CHALLENGE** Describe a method for finding the center and scale factor of a dilation that moves a given circle onto another given circle with a different radius.

30. ★ **EXTENDED RESPONSE** The figure below shows an architect's initial layout of the floor plan for a house. The scale is $\frac{1}{2}$ inch = 1 foot.

a. **Interpret** How is a dilation of the floor plan used in the house construction? What is the scale factor of the dilation?

b. **Model** Explain how to find the actual size of the living room in the house using the floor plan.

c. **Calculate** Find the actual size of each room in the house.

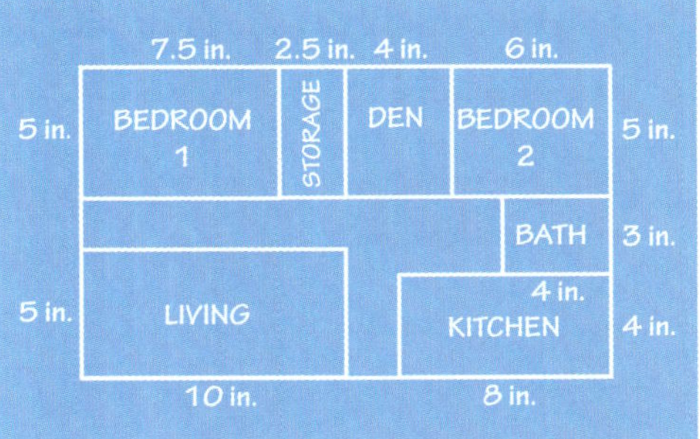

31. ★ **OPEN-ENDED** A transformation in the coordinate plane is described using the notation $(x, y) \rightarrow (2x, 5y)$. *Explain* why the transformation is not a similarity transformation by showing how it affects the angles and sides of a polygon.

32. **CHALLENGE** A dilation of a triangle is shown, in which the center of dilation lies in the interior of the triangle.

a. Use the slope formula to show that corresponding sides are parallel.

b. The black rays in the diagram are transversals that intersect parallel segments. Prove the angles marked are congruent. *Explain* why the angles of the preimage and image triangles are preserved under the dilation.

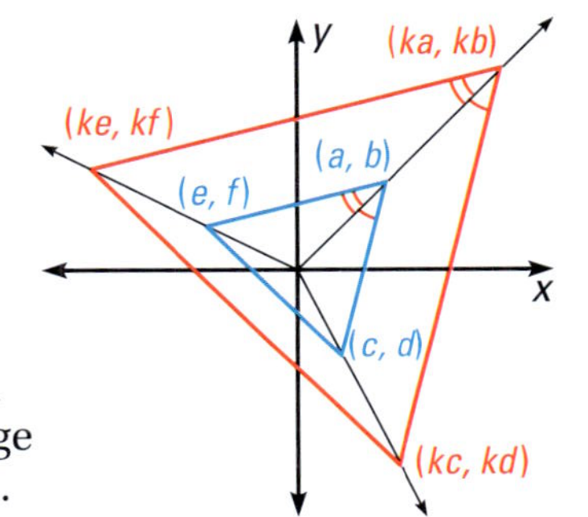

PREVIEW
Prepare for
Lesson 6.4
in Exs. 33–36

Write a congruence statement for the triangles. Identify all pairs of congruent corresponding parts. *(Lesson 4.2)*

33. 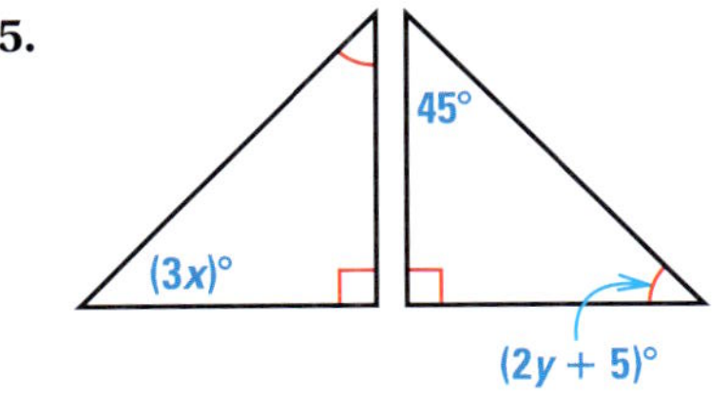

34. 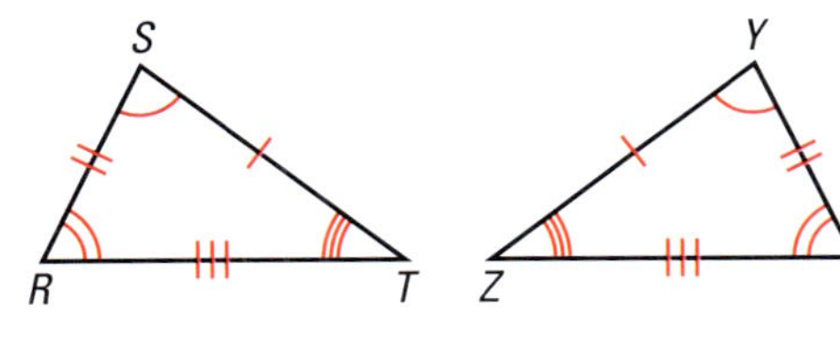

Find the values of x and y. *(Lesson 4.2)*

35. 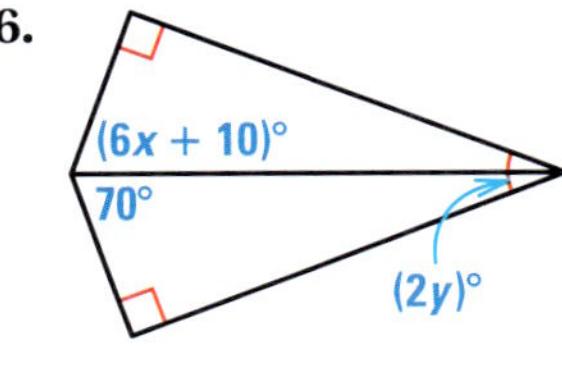

36. 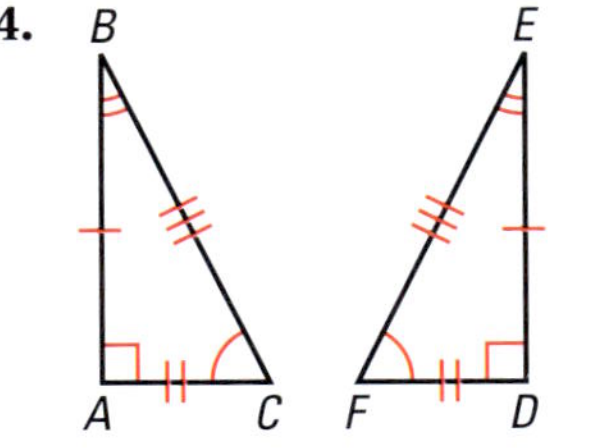

Is it possible to construct a triangle with the given side lengths? If not, *explain* why not. *(Lesson 5.5)*

37. 4, 5, 9   38. 2, 8, 9   39. 20, 20, 45

6.4 Dilations and AA Similarity

MATERIALS • ruler • protractor

QUESTION How can you use a dilation to map a triangle onto a similar triangle with two pairs of corresponding angles congruent?

Recall that a dilation preserves angle measures but not lengths.

EXPLORE Build similar triangles given two angles

STEP 1 *Draw triangles* Draw $\triangle ABC$ with any angles. Use a protractor to draw a larger $\triangle DEF$, with $\angle D \cong \angle A$ and $\angle E \cong \angle B$. Inside $\triangle DEF$, draw a segment parallel to $\overline{DE}$ the same length as $\overline{AB}$. Label its endpoints G and H.

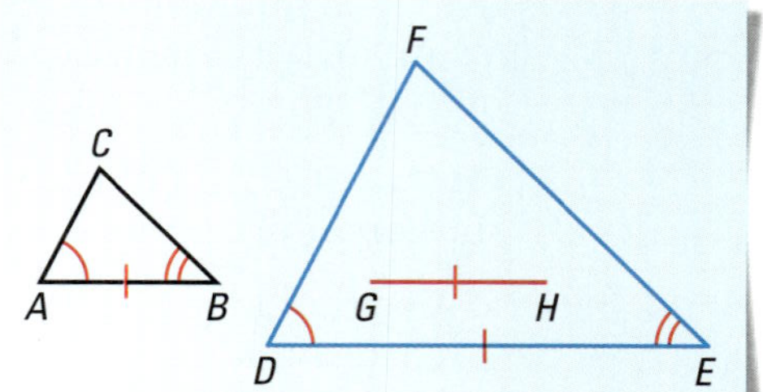

STEP 2 *Copy angles* Copy $\angle D$ at G and copy $\angle E$ at H. Extend the sides until they intersect. Label the intersection J.

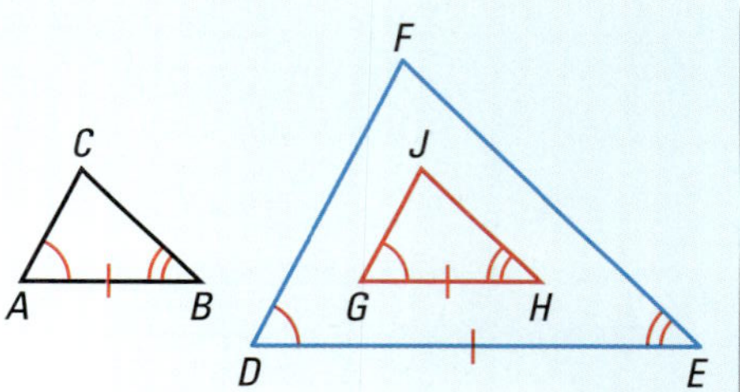

STEP 3 *Find center of dilation* Draw three rays that intersect: $\overrightarrow{DG}$, $\overrightarrow{EH}$, and $\overrightarrow{FJ}$. Label their point of intersection O.

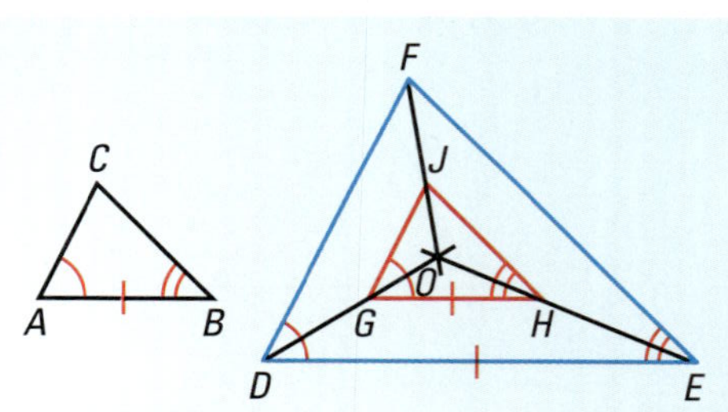

DRAW CONCLUSIONS Use your observations to complete these exercises

1. Measure $\angle C$, $\angle F$, and $\angle J$. What do you notice?

2. A dilation maps $\triangle DEF$ to $\triangle GHJ$. Why is $\angle D \cong \angle G$ and $\angle E \cong \angle H$?

3. Find $\dfrac{GO}{DO}$, $\dfrac{HO}{EO}$, and $\dfrac{JO}{FO}$. What is the scale factor of the dilation?

4. Prove that $\triangle GHJ \cong \triangle ABC$. *Justify* your reasoning.

5. What combination of transformations maps $\triangle DEF$ to $\triangle ABC$?

Mastering the Standards

for Mathematical Practice

The topics described in the Standards for Mathematical Content will vary from year to year. However, the *way* in which you learn, study, and think about mathematics will not. The Standards for Mathematical Practice describe skills that you will use in all of your math courses.

Mathematical Practices

1. *Make sense of problems and persevere in solving them.*
2. *Reason abstractly and quantitatively.*
3. *Construct viable arguments and critique the reasoning of others.*
4. Model with mathematics.
5. *Use appropriate tools strategically.*
6. *Attend to precision.*
7. *Look for and make use of structure.*
8. *Look for and express regularity in repeated reasoning.*

4 Model with mathematics.

Mathematically proficient students can apply... mathematics... to... problems... in everyday life, society, and the workplace...

In your book

Application exercises and **Mixed Reviews of Problem Solving** apply mathematics to other disciplines and in real-world scenarios.

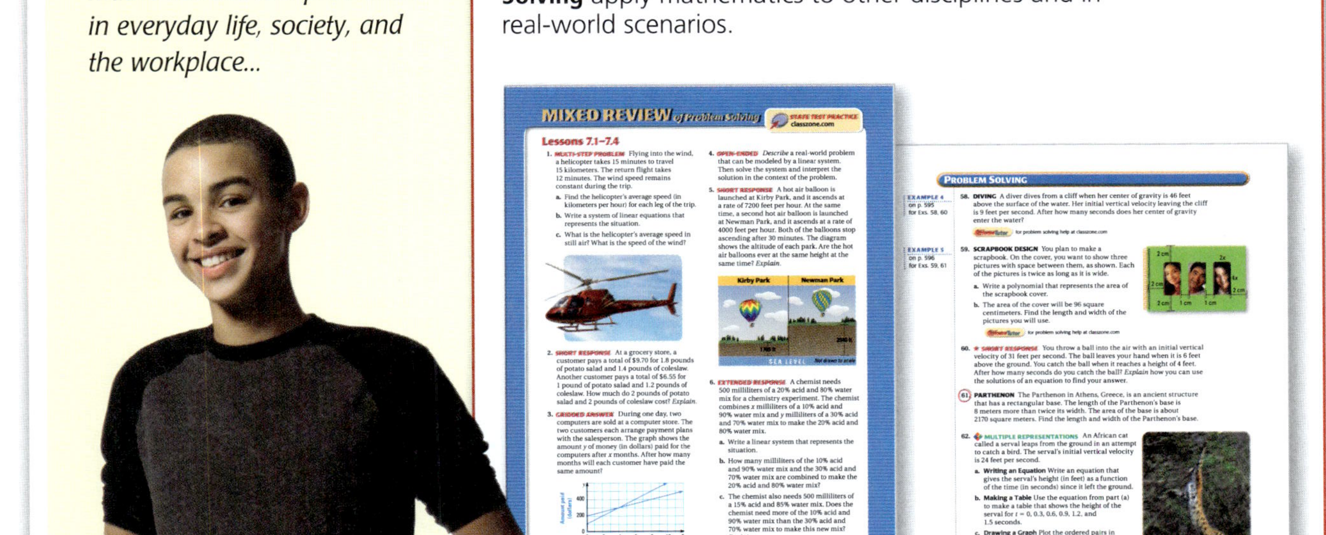

Extension
Use after Lesson 6.7

Partition Segments

GOAL Find the point that partitions a directed line segment in a given ratio.

Recall that the *slope* of a nonvertical line is the ratio of *rise* (the vertical change) to *run* (the horizontal change) between any two points on the line.

$$\text{slope} = \frac{\text{rise}}{\text{run}}$$

A *directed line segment AB* is a segment that represents moving from point A to point B. The following example shows how to use slope to find a point at a specific location on a directed line segment.

EXAMPLE 1   Find a point along a directed line segment

Find the coordinates of point P along the directed line segment AB so that the ratio of AP to PB is 3 to 2.

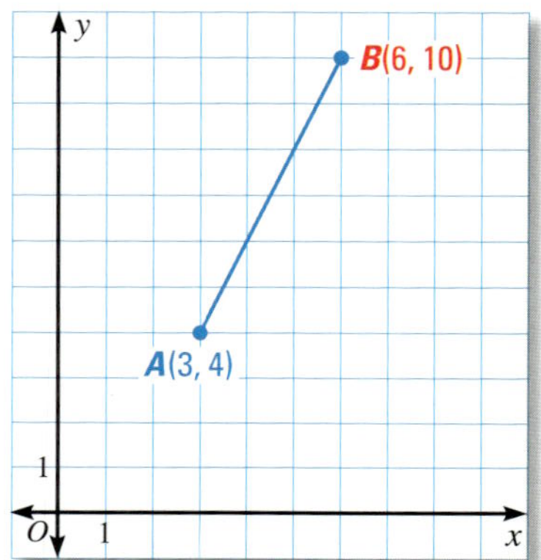

Solution

In order to divide the segment in the ratio 3 to 2, think of dividing, or *partitioning*, the segment into $3 + 2$, or 5 congruent pieces.

Point P is the point that is $\frac{3}{5}$ of the way *from* point A to point B.

The diagram shows the rise and run from point A to point B.

$$\text{slope of } \overline{AB} = \frac{10 - 4}{6 - 3} = \frac{6}{3} = \frac{\text{rise}}{\text{run}}$$

To find the coordinates of point P, add $\frac{3}{5}$ of the run to the x-coordinate of A, and add $\frac{3}{5}$ of the rise to the y-coordinate of A.

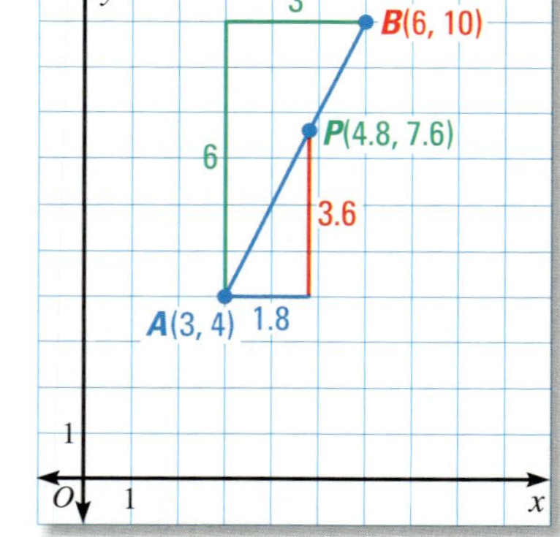

run: $\frac{3}{5}$ of 3 = **1.8**

rise: $\frac{3}{5}$ of 6 = **3.6**

▶ So, the coordinates of P are $(3 + 1.8, 4 + 3.6) = (4.8, 7.6)$. The ratio of AP to PB is 3 to 2.

EXAMPLE 2 Construct a point along a directed line segment

Construct the point L on $\overline{AB}$ so that the ratio of AL to LB is 3 to 1.

Solution

STEP 1 **Draw** $\overline{AB}$ of any length. Choose any point C not on $\overleftrightarrow{AB}$. Draw $\overrightarrow{AC}$.

STEP 2 **Place** the point of a compass at A and make an arc of any radius intersecting $\overrightarrow{AC}$ at D. Using the same compass setting, make three more arcs on $\overrightarrow{AC}$ as shown. Label the points of intersection E, F, and G, and note that $AD = DE = EF = FG$.

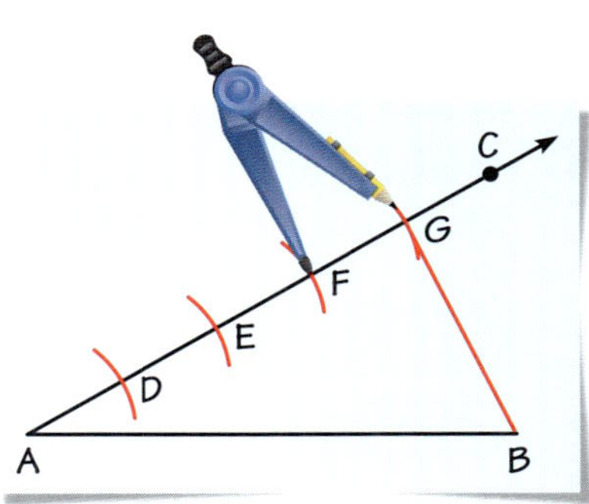

STEP 3 **Draw** $\overline{GB}$. Use the copy an angle construction to copy $\angle AGB$ at D, E, and F. The new sides are all parallel, and they intersect $\overline{AB}$ at J, K, and L, dividing $\overline{AB}$ equally, so that $AJ = JK = KL = LB$.

▶ Point L divides directed line segment AB in the ratio 3 to 1.

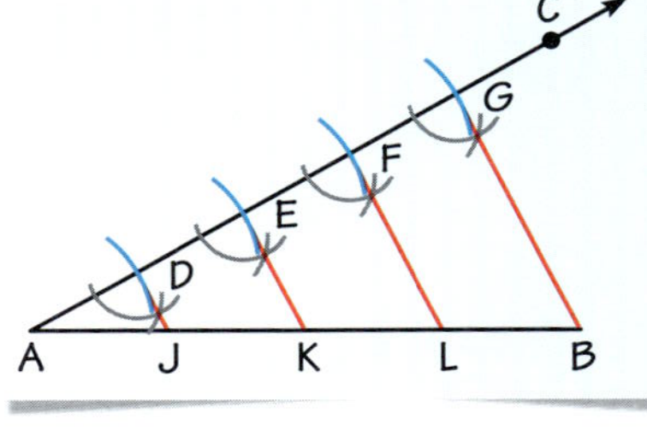

PRACTICE

EXAMPLE 1
on p. CC22
for Exs. 1–4

PARTITIONING Find the coordinates of point P along the directed line segment AB so that AP to PB is the given ratio.

1. $A(1, 3)$, $B(8, 4)$; 4 to 1

2. $A(-2, 1)$, $B(4, 5)$; 3 to 7

3. $A(8, 0)$, $B(3, -2)$; 1 to 4

4. $A(-2, -4)$, $B(6, 1)$; 3 to 2

EXAMPLE 2
on p. CC23
for Exs. 5–8

CONSTRUCTION Draw a segment with the given length. Construct the point that divides the segment in the given ratio.

5. length: 3 in.; ratio: 1 to 4

6. length: 2 in.; ratio: 2 to 3

7. length: 12 cm; ratio: 1 to 3

8. length: 9 cm; ratio: 2 to 5

9. REASONING In Example 2, what theorem helps you to conclude that $AJ = JK = KL = LB$? *Explain.*

10. VISUALIZATION Suppose point P divides $\overline{XY}$ so that XP to PY is 3 to 5. Describe the point that divides $\overline{YX}$ so that YP to PX is 5 to 3.

11. WHAT IF? Make a conjecture about how to find the coordinates of a point that lies beyond point B along $\overrightarrow{AB}$. Use an example to support your conjecture.

10.4 Tangent Lines and Inscribed Squares

MATERIALS • compass • straightedge

QUESTION What constructions use right angles inscribed in circles?

Recall that in a plane, a line is tangent to a circle if and only if the line is perpendicular to a radius of the circle at its endpoint on the circle.

EXPLORE 1 Construct a tangent to a circle

STEP 1 *Find midpoint* Given $\odot C$ and point A, draw $\overline{AC}$. Construct the bisector of the segment and label the midpoint M.

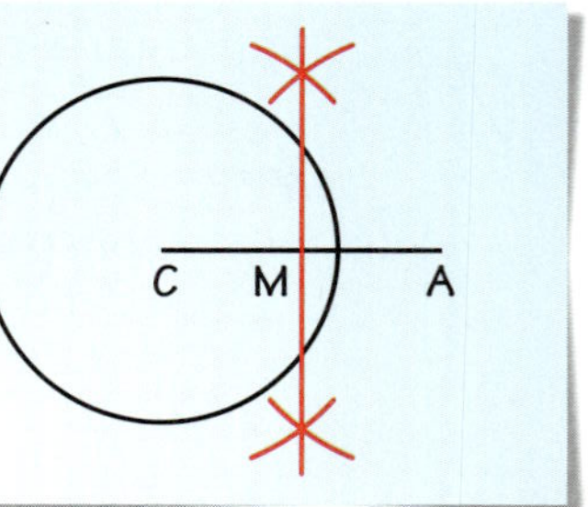

STEP 2 *Draw circle* Construct $\odot M$ with radius MA. Label one of the points where $\odot M$ intersects $\odot C$ as point B.

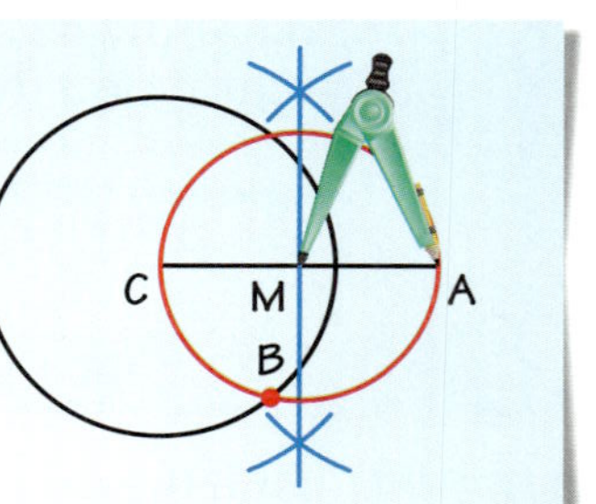

STEP 3 *Construct tangent* Draw $\overleftrightarrow{AB}$. It is the tangent to $\odot C$ that passes through A.

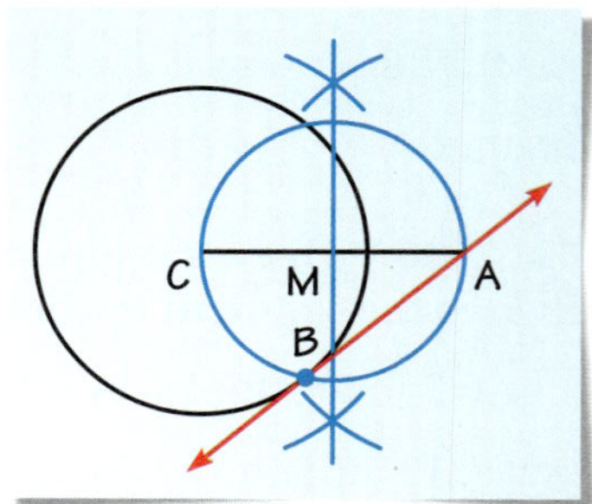

DRAW CONCLUSIONS Use your observations to complete these exercises

1. Explain how to construct the other tangent to $\odot C$ from point A.

2. Add $\overline{BC}$ to your construction. *Explain* how $\triangle ABC$ can be used to prove that $\overleftrightarrow{AB}$ is a tangent to $\odot C$.

3. Can $\odot M$ be *larger* than $\odot C$ in the construction of a tangent? If so, *describe* under what conditions this can occur.

An inscribed polygon is a polygon that has all of its vertices on a circle.
So, an inscribed square must have all four of its vertices on the circle.

EXPLORE 2 Construct a square inscribed in a circle

STEP 1 *Draw diameter* Given ⊙C, draw any diameter.
Label the endpoints A and B.

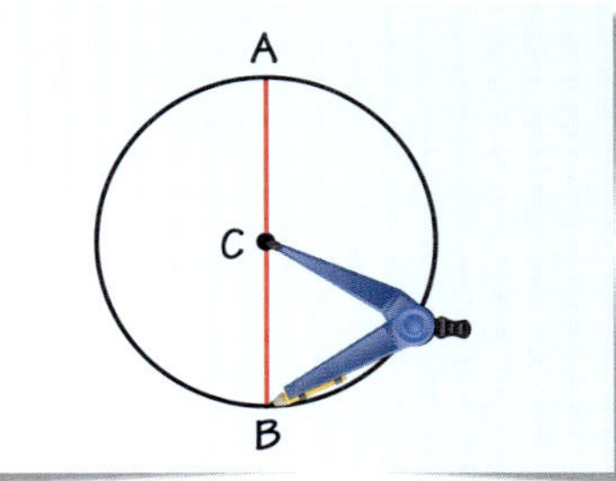

STEP 2 *Construct bisector* Construct the bisector of
the diameter. Label the points where it
intersects ⊙C as points D and E.

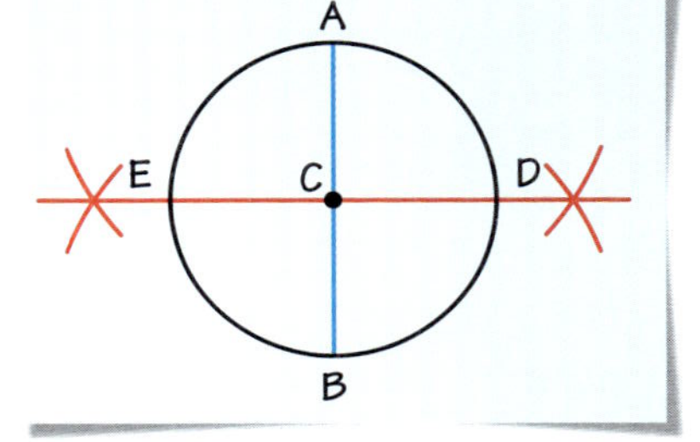

STEP 3 *Form square* Connect points A, D, B, and E to
form square $ADBE$.

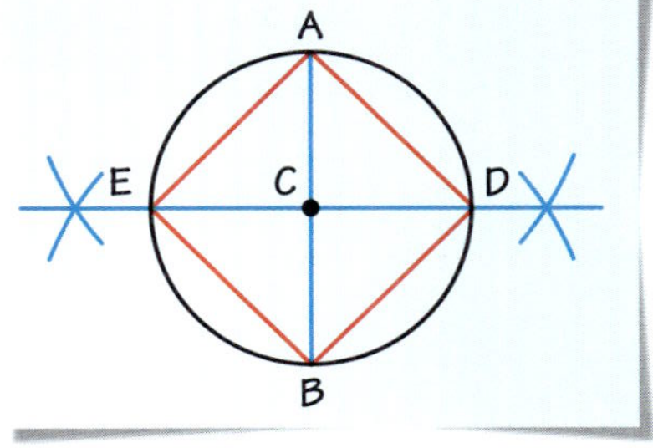

DRAW CONCLUSIONS Use your observations to complete these exercises

4. In Explore 2, Step 2, why can you conclude that $\overleftrightarrow{DE} \perp \overleftrightarrow{AB}$?

5. Show that $ADBE$ is a rectangle by proving it has four right angles.

6. Show that $ADBE$ is a rhombus by proving it has four congruent sides.

7. How do you know quadrilateral $ADBE$ is a square?

8. Is a quadrilateral that is inscribed in a circle always a square? *Explain* why or why not.

9. Tell how you might extend the construction in Explore 2 to construct an inscribed regular octagon in ⊙C.

10. Tell how you might extend the construction in Explore 2 to inscribe a circle in the square in ⊙C.

Mastering the Standards

for Mathematical Practice

The topics described in the Standards for Mathematical Content will vary from year to year. However, the *way* in which you learn, study, and think about mathematics will not. The Standards for Mathematical Practice describe skills that you will use in all of your math courses.

Mathematical Practices

1. Make sense of problems and persevere in solving them.
2. Reason abstractly and quantitatively.
3. Construct viable arguments and critique the reasoning of others.
4. Model with mathematics.
5. Use appropriate tools strategically.
6. Attend to precision.
7. Look for and make use of structure.
8. Look for and express regularity in repeated reasoning.

5 Use appropriate tools strategically.

Mathematically proficient students consider the available tools when solving a... problem... [and] are... able to use technological tools to explore and deepen their understanding...

In your book

Problem Solving Workshops explore alternative methods as tools for problem solving. A variety of **Activities** use concrete and technological tools to explore mathematical concepts.

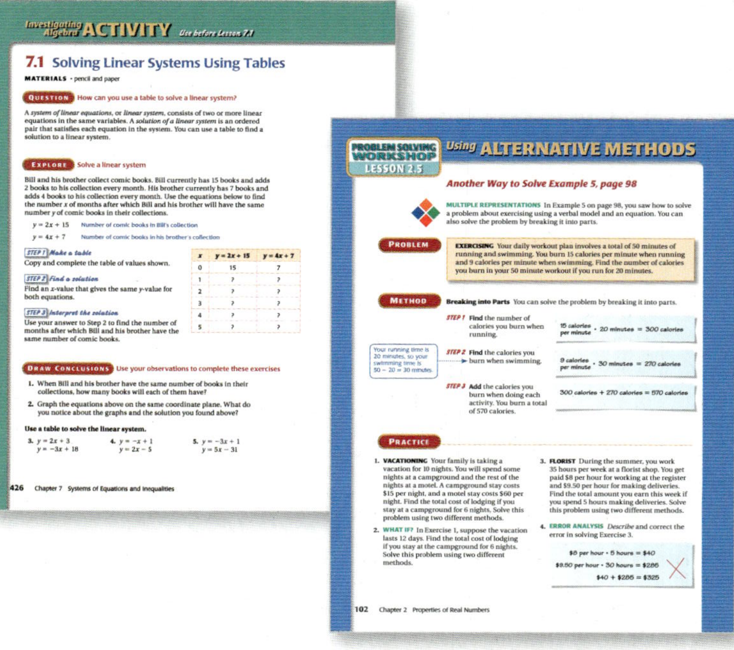

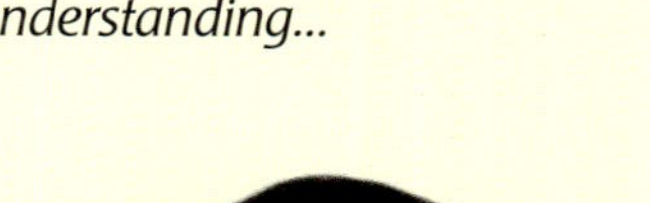

Measure Angles in Radians

GOAL Find the radian measure of an angle.

Key Vocabulary
• radian

In the Activity below, you will explore the relationship between radii and arc length for a central angle of concentric circles.

ACTIVITY CONSTANT OF PROPORTIONALITY

STEP 1 **Find** the lengths of the arcs intercepted by a central angle of 60° for four concentric circles with radii 1, 2, 3, and 4.

Radius	Arc Length Calculation	Arc Length
1	$\dfrac{m\widehat{AB}}{360°} \cdot 2\pi r = \dfrac{60°}{360°} \cdot 2\pi \cdot 1 = \dfrac{\pi}{3}$	$\dfrac{\pi}{3}$
2	?	?
3	?	?
4	?	?

STEP 2 **Explain** how to express the arc length as a direct variation.

STEP 3 **Make** a conjecture about what happens to the arc length if the radius is doubled.

In a circle, the ratio of the length of a given arc to the circumference is equal to the ratio of the measure of the arc to 360°, and therefore

$$\text{arc length of } \widehat{AB} = \frac{m\widehat{AB}}{360°} \cdot 2\pi r$$

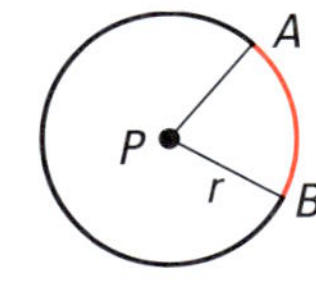

The form of this equation shows that the arc length associated with a central angle is *proportional to the radius* of the circle.

The constant of proportionality, $\dfrac{m\widehat{AB}}{360°} \cdot 2\pi$, is defined to be the **radian** measure of the central angle associated with the arc.

The radian measure can be thought of as the length of the arc associated with a given central angle in a circle of radius 1.

CONVERSION The radian measure of a complete circle (360°) is exactly 2π radians, because the circumference of a circle of radius 1 is exactly 2π. You can use this fact to convert from degree measure to radian measure and vice versa.

To convert from degree measure to radian measure, use this relationship:

$$\text{degree measure} \cdot \frac{2\pi}{360°} = \text{radian measure}$$

To convert from radian measure to degree measure, use this relationship:

$$\text{radian measure} \cdot \frac{360°}{2\pi} = \text{degree measure}$$

EXAMPLE   **Convert between degree and radian measure**

  a. Convert 45° to radians.   **b.** Convert $\frac{3\pi}{2}$ radians to degrees.

Solution

a. $45° \cdot \dfrac{2\pi}{360°} = \dfrac{1}{4}\pi$ or $\dfrac{\pi}{4}$ **b.** $\dfrac{3\pi}{2} \cdot \dfrac{360°}{2\pi} = 270°$

  So, $45° = \dfrac{\pi}{4}$ radians.   So, $\dfrac{3\pi}{2}$ radians $= 270°$.

PRACTICE

ACTIVITY
on p. CC27
for Exs. 1–3

ARC LENGTH Find the length of the arc associated with the given central angle and radius.

1. 120°; radius 4   **2.** 135°; radius 1.5   **3.** 240°; radius 3

CONVERSION Convert the degree measure to radian measure.

4. 15°   **5.** 70°   **6.** 300°

EXAMPLE
on p. CC28
for Exs. 4–10

CONVERSION Convert the radian measure to degree measure.

7. $\dfrac{4\pi}{3}$ radians   **8.** $\dfrac{11\pi}{12}$ radians   **9.** $\dfrac{\pi}{8}$ radians

10. Copy and complete the table by giving the equivalent degree or radian measure of the benchmark arcs.

Degrees	30°	45°	?	?	120°	?	?	?	360°
Radians	?	?	$\dfrac{\pi}{3}$	$\dfrac{\pi}{2}$	?	$\dfrac{3\pi}{4}$	π	$\dfrac{3\pi}{2}$	?

11. The arc length on a circle can be also be found using the formula $s = r \cdot \theta$, where s is the arc length, r is the radius of the circle, and θ is the central angle (measured in radians) associated with the arc. Find the length of an arc in a circle when the radius is 4 inches and the central angle is $\dfrac{3\pi}{4}$ radians.

Mastering *the* Standards

for Mathematical Practice

The topics described in the Standards for Mathematical Content will vary from year to year. However, the *way* in which you learn, study, and think about mathematics will not. The Standards for Mathematical Practice describe skills that you will use in all of your math courses.

Mathematical Practices

1. *Make sense of problems and persevere in solving them.*
2. *Reason abstractly and quantitatively.*
3. *Construct viable arguments and critique the reasoning of others.*
4. *Model with mathematics.*
5. *Use appropriate tools strategically.*
6. *Attend to precision.*
7. *Look for and make use of structure.*
8. *Look for and express regularity in repeated reasoning.*

1 **Make sense of problems and persevere in solving them.**

Mathematically proficient students start by explaining to themselves the meaning of a problem... They analyze givens, constraints, relationships, and goals. They make conjectures about the form... of the solution and plan a solution pathway...

In your book

Verbal Models and the **Problem Solving Plan** help you translate the information in a problem into a model and then analyze your solution.

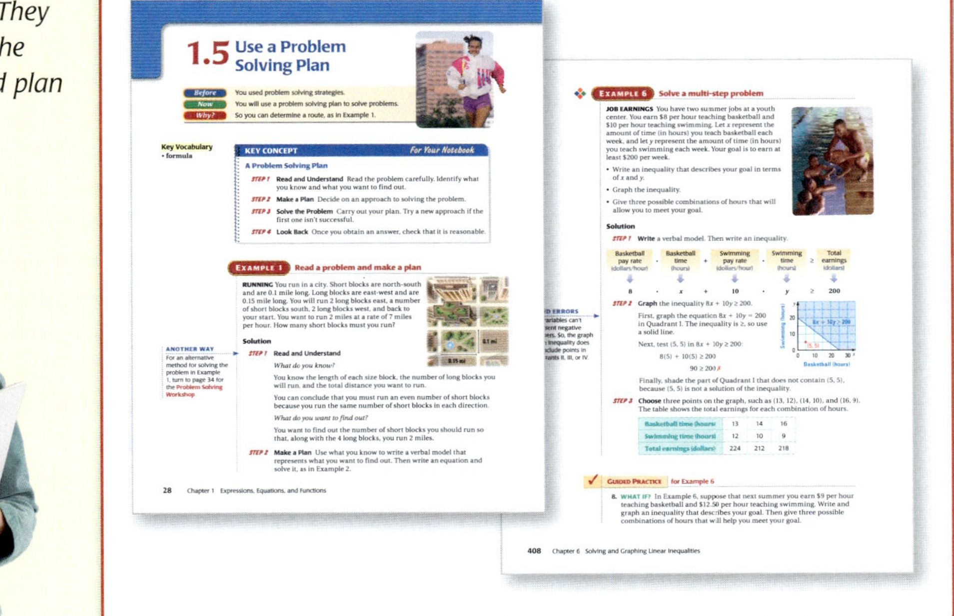

Density

GOAL Use density to solve problems.

Key Vocabulary
- density
- population density

Density is the amount of matter that an object has in a given unit of volume. The density of an object is calculated by dividing its mass by its volume.

$$\text{density} = \frac{\text{mass}}{\text{volume}}$$

Different materials have different densities, so density can be used to distinguish between materials that look similar. For example, table salt and sugar look alike. However, table salt has a density of 2.16 grams per cubic centimeter, while sugar has a density of 1.58 grams per cubic centimeter.

EXAMPLE 1 Determine which substance has greater density

A piece of copper with a volume of 8.25 cubic centimeters has a mass of 73.92 grams. A piece of iron with a volume of 5 cubic centimeters has a mass of 39.35 grams. Which metal has the greater density?

Solution

Calculate the density of each metal.

Copper: $\text{density} = \dfrac{\text{mass}}{\text{volume}} = \dfrac{73.92 \text{ g}}{8.25 \text{ cm}^3} = 8.96 \text{ g/cm}^3$

Iron: $\text{density} = \dfrac{\text{mass}}{\text{volume}} = \dfrac{39.35 \text{ g}}{5 \text{ cm}^3} = 7.87 \text{ g/cm}^3$

▶ Copper has the greater density.

POPULATION DENSITY Another use of the word density occurs in the term population density. The **population density** of a city, county, or state is a measure of how many people live within a given area.

$$\text{population density} = \frac{\text{number of people}}{\text{area of land}}$$

Population density is usually given in terms of square miles, but can be expressed using other units such as city blocks.

The population of Vermont in 2009 was 621,760. The state can be modeled by a trapezoid with vertices at (0, 0), (0, 160), (80, 160), and (40, 0), with each unit on the coordinate plane being 1 mile. Find the population density of Vermont.

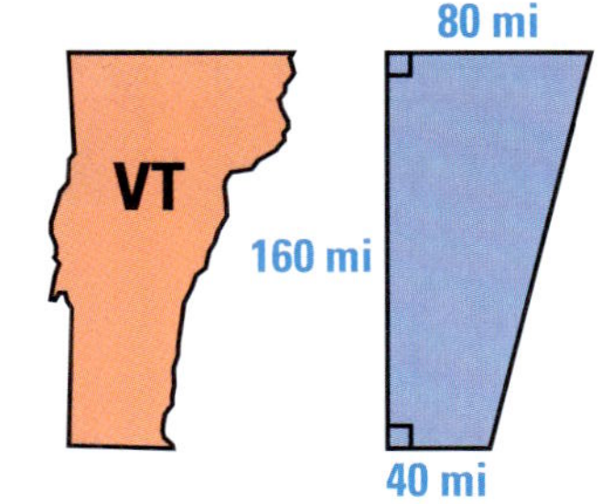

Solution

STEP 1   **Sketch** the simplified model of Vermont.

STEP 2   **Calculate** the area of the trapezoid. The height is 160 miles and the bases have length 80 miles and 40 miles.

$$A = \tfrac{1}{2}h(b_1 + b_2) = \tfrac{1}{2}(160)(80 + 40) = 9600 \text{ mi}^2$$

STEP 3   **Find** the population density.

$$\text{density} = \frac{\text{number of people}}{\text{area of land}} = \frac{621{,}760 \text{ people}}{9600 \text{ mi}^2} \approx 64.8 \text{ people/mi}^2$$

▶ In 2009, there were about 65 people per square mile living in Vermont.

PRACTICE

EXAMPLE 1
on p. CC30
for Ex. 1

1. **METALS** Toni found an irregular piece of metal. She dropped it into a container partially filled with water and measured that the water level rose 4.8 centimeters. The square base of the container is 8 centimeters on a side. Toni measures the mass of the metal to be 450 grams. What is the density of the metal? Round to the nearest tenth.

EXAMPLE 2
on p. CC31
for Exs. 2–3

2. **POPULATION DENSITY** The population of Colorado in 2009 was about 5,024,748. The land area can be approximated by a rectangle with coordinates (0, 0), (369, 0), (369, 281), and (0, 281), with each unit on the coordinate plane being 1 mile. What was the population density of Colorado in 2009?

3. **POPULATION DENSITY** In 2000, Texas had about 2.74 persons per household, 7,393,354 households, and a land area of about 261,797 square miles. What was the population density of Texas in 2000? If the population in 2009 was about 24,782,302, how did the density in 2009 compare to the density in 2000?

4. **COOLING** On average during the summer, a 30,000 cubic foot house costs $7 per day to cool, while a 25,000 cubic foot house costs $6.50 per day to cool. Which house costs less per cubic foot to cool? *Explain.*

5. **REASONING** If two objects have the same volume, which object has a greater mass, the heavier object or the lighter object? *Explain.*

Solids of Revolution

GOAL Sketch and describe solids produced by rotating a two-dimensional figure around an axis in space.

Key Vocabulary
• solid of revolution
• axis of revolution

A **solid of revolution** is a three-dimensional figure that is formed by rotating a two-dimensional shape around an axis. The line around which the shape is rotated is called the **axis of revolution**.

For example, if you rotate a rectangle around a line that contains one of its sides, the solid of revolution that is produced is a cylinder.

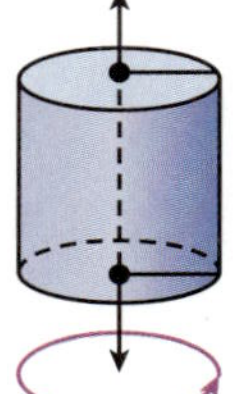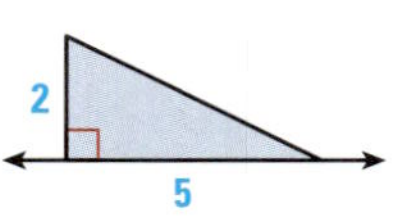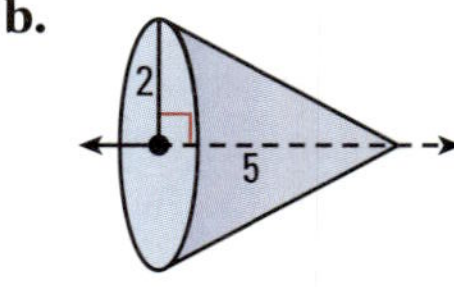

EXAMPLE 1 Sketch and describe a solid of revolution

Sketch the solid produced by rotating the figure around the given axis. Then identify and describe the solid.

a.
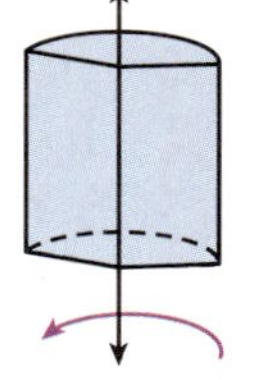

b.
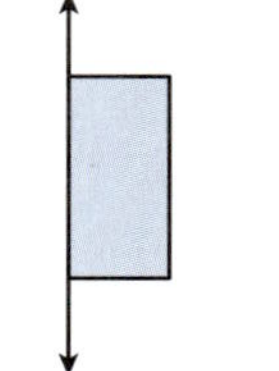

Solution

a.
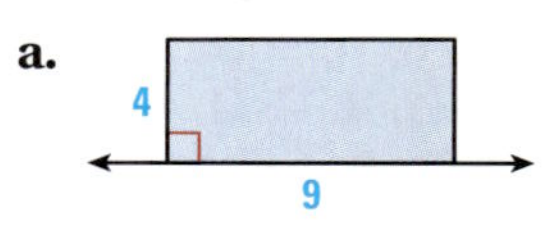

Cylinder with height 9 and base radius 4

b.
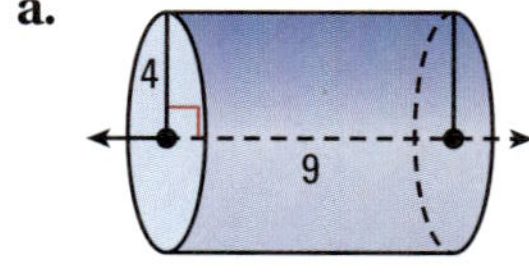

Cone with height 5 and base radius 2

Because the dimensions of the original figure can be used to describe the solid of revolution, you can use these dimensions to calculate the volume of the solid of revolution.

EXAMPLE 2   Find the volume of a solid of revolution

Sketch the solid produced by rotating the figure around the given axis. Then find its volume.

a. 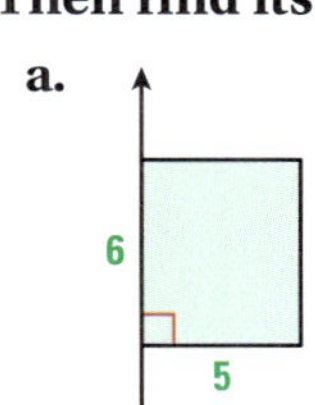

b. 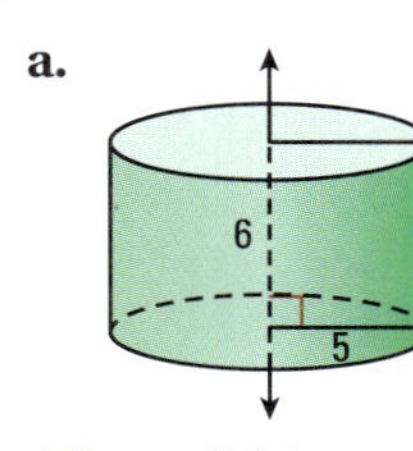

Solution

a. 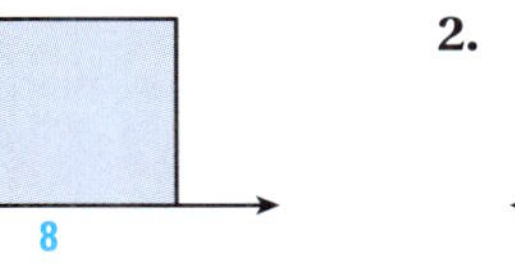

b. 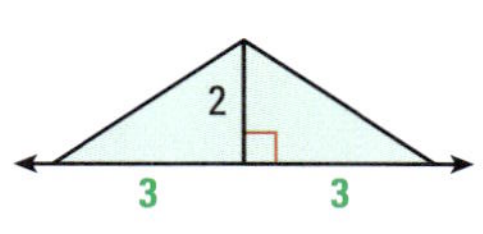

The solid is a cylinder with height 6 and base radius 5.

$$V = \pi r^2 h = \pi(5^2)(6) = 150\pi$$

The solid is made of two cones, each with height 3 and base radius 2.

$$V = 2 \cdot \frac{1}{3}\pi r^2 h = 2 \cdot \frac{1}{3}\pi(2^2)(3) = 8\pi$$

PRACTICE

EXAMPLE 1
on p. CC32
for Exs. 1–6

Sketch the solid produced by rotating the figure around the given axis. Then identify and describe the solid.

1. 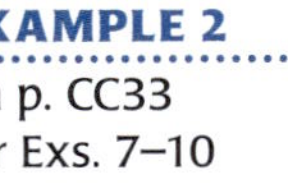

2.

3.

Sketch the solid of revolution. Then identify and describe the solid.

4. A square with side length 4 rotated around one side.

5. A rectangle with length 5 and width 2 rotated around its longer side.

6. A right triangle with legs of length 6 and 9 rotated around its shorter leg.

EXAMPLE 2
on p. CC33
for Exs. 7–10

Sketch the solid produced by rotating the figure around the given axis. Then find its volume.

7. 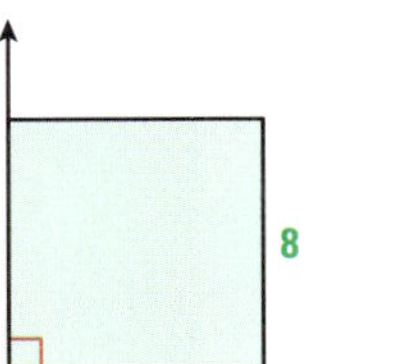

8. 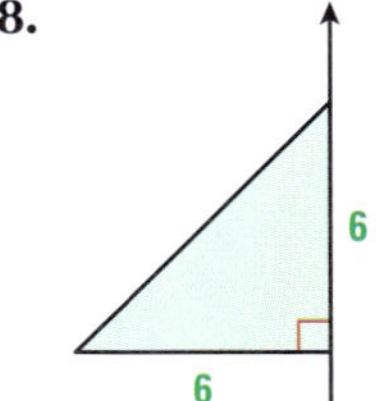

9. 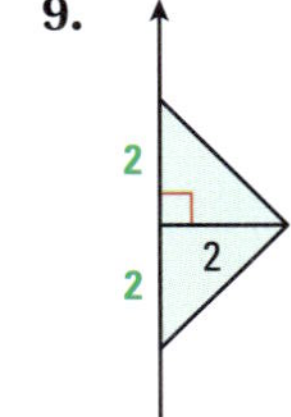

10. **CHALLENGE** A 30°-30°-120° isosceles triangle has two legs of length 4 units. If it is rotated around an axis that contains one leg, what is the volume of the solid of revolution?